# CONTENTS

D0453067

# Introduction

**Child Abuse** is the one hundred and thirty-second volume in the **Issues** series. The aim of this series is to offer up-to-date information about important issues in our world.

**Child Abuse** looks at the various issues surrounding child abuse, the debate regarding smacking, and the problem of child sexual abuse.

The information comes from a wide variety of sources and includes:
Government reports and statistics
Newspaper reports and features
Magazine articles and surveys
Website material
Literature from lobby groups
and charitable organisations.

It is hoped that, as you read about the many aspects of the issues explored in this book, you will critically evaluate the information presented. It is important that you decide whether you are being presented with facts or opinions. Does the writer give a biased or an unbiased report? If an opinion is being expressed, do you agree with the writer?

**Child Abuse** offers a useful starting-point for those who need convenient access to information about the many issues involved. However, it is only a starting-point. Following each article is a URL to the relevant organisation's website, which you may wish to visit for further information.

\* \* \* \* \*

# Child abuse

## Information taken from a ChildLine information sheet

*'I was nine years old when it started. Sexual abuse and stuff like that. After it stopped, I still felt awful. I couldn't bear it and just wanted to die. I took a whole bottle of tablets and ended up in hospital. Then I saw a poster about ChildLine, and decided to call. When I went into the phone box I was so scared. I felt so bad about telling on him. The counsellor had this gentle voice, so I started telling her. I went on calling ChildLine for a year after it all came out. Now I'm nearly 20. I don't talk about it much any more, but I'd like to nominate my ChildLine counsellor for an award.' Sara, 19*

Every child has the right to grow up in a caring and safe environment. Fortunately most children and young people do. They receive the love and care they need to develop into healthy, happy adults.

But not all.

Some children are not loved by their families. Others live in families that are having a really difficult time and cannot cope with their problems. Some children are deliberately neglected or hurt by the adults around them.

### What is child abuse?

Abuse can take different forms and a child may suffer from more than one form at a time. These are:
⇨ sexual abuse
⇨ physical abuse
⇨ emotional abuse
⇨ neglect.

### 1. SEXUAL ABUSE

*'I thought for a long time that what was happening was OK because Dad said that it was a game people played with their sons – a secret game that only men knew about.' Adrian, 15*

Sexual abuse is when a child takes part in sexual activities – whether or not the child is aware of what is happening. These activities can include being forced or lured to have sex; touching or being touched in a way that makes a child uncomfortable; or encouraging children to behave in sexual ways that other children of their age would not do. Abuse also includes children looking at or producing sexual images, known as pornography.

### 2. PHYSICAL ABUSE

*'Yesterday I spent my dinner money on a McDonald's with my friends. When my mum found out she went mad. She called me a thief and punched me until my nose bled. It felt like she wanted to kill me. Mum and Dad both beat me with anything they can find – shoes, plates and coat hangers.' Tracey, 10*

Physical abuse is when a child is hurt by being smacked, hit, kicked, or shaken; beaten by hand, with a belt or other objects; or physically abused in other ways. Children have told ChildLine of hiding bruises from teachers and friends, being taken to the hospital with broken bones, and of suffering cuts, burns and other injuries.

### 3. EMOTIONAL ABUSE

*'Dad shouts at me a lot. I hate it when he gets angry. It makes me feel shaky and awful inside. I want to tell my dad how I feel, but I'm scared he won't listen to me.' Chris, 8*

Emotional abuse is when children do not feel loved or valued because they are constantly told off, put down or told they are no good at anything. Some children tell ChildLine's counsellors that they are criticised, shouted and sworn at, persistently blamed for things they have no control over, or told that other people – sometimes brothers or sisters – are better than they are. When children are emotionally abused, they are turned away when they need love or support, and are frequently rejected or ignored by those who are meant to look after them.

### 4. NEGLECT

*'My mum and dad are alcoholics. I've run away a few times and they always say they worry about me, but they never do anything about it. They spend all the money on drink. There's no soap in the house and all my clothes are too small. All the kids in my class call me names and make fun of me. It hurts.' Paul, 14*

Neglect is when children are denied the essentials in life they need to grow up and become healthy, well-cared-for adults. Neglected children are forced to get by without proper food, housing, medical care or clothing. They can miss going to school and not be able to mix with their friends and peers. Also they may not be

properly protected by their parents or carers from physical or mental harm. Neglected children can be hungry, cold, lonely and sick.

### How many children are abused?

It is impossible to know how many children are abused. ChildLine is for any child with any problem, but the largest number of calls we receive are about abuse.

---

## Calling ChildLine gives children the opportunity to talk to someone 'safe'

---

Every year, ChildLine receives tens of thousands of calls from children who are frightened, shocked and in terrible distress because of the abuse they have suffered. Each call is an act of courage that will change a child's life. In 2001/02, ChildLine counselled over 112,000 children about all kinds of problems and concerns:

⇨ 21,000 of children counselled (20 per cent) rang about physical or sexual abuse, sometimes both
⇨ over 12,400 of those children were counselled about physical abuse
⇨ over 8,400 of those children were counselled about sexual abuse.

ChildLine has been at the forefront of changing public awareness in the UK about child sexual abuse. Our approach to children calling about abuse remains the same today as when we launched. The helpline counsellors aim to support children and young people with information, with choices and with emotional support – to build their confidence, so that they realise they are not to blame and that they have the right to be safe.

### My dad hits me all the time. What am I doing wrong?

You are doing nothing wrong. It is not your fault if you are abused – physically, sexually or emotionally – or if you are neglected. All children are naughty or get into trouble sometimes, but that does not give adults the right to abuse them. It is the abuser who is wrong.

If children or young people are sexually abused, their bodies can sometimes respond in ways that can make them feel ashamed. This is not their fault. It is the fault of the abuser.

All children have a right to be safe. They should not have to keep secrets and should not have to deal with abuse on their own.

If you are being abused or neglected – or believe you are at risk of being abused – you must think of someone you trust, like a parent, teacher, relative or friend, and tell them. You have a right to be believed. If the first person you tell doesn't believe you or won't help, then you should find someone else to talk to or phone ChildLine. You have a right to be helped.

Every week ChildLine counsellors talk to children who are being threatened, assaulted and raped. Their experiences are so acutely degrading – and frightening – that just for children to talk about them is difficult. Without ChildLine many children would simply be too afraid to get help. Most children calling about abuse are between 13 and 15 years old.

ChildLine offers something completely unique to thousands of children and young people who feel they have nowhere to turn. They know they will be listened to. This simple fact means that children know they can get help and so are asking for help earlier by calling ChildLine.

ChildLine has played a vital role in helping ensure that children are far more likely to be believed when they disclose abuse. Increasingly children themselves realise they have the right to be safe.

### I've been touched in a way that makes me uncomfortable. Am I being abused?

Abuse can take many forms. It can also mean different things to different children. Some children, especially younger ones, may be abused without knowing that what is happening to them is wrong.

A child or young person may experience one form of abuse, like emotional abuse. Alternatively they may suffer more than one form of abuse at a time. For example, a

young person may be sexually and emotionally abused.

Abuse can happen once or it can occur many times. Either way, the abused person needs to seek help.

### Who abuses children?

Many people, including children, believe that they are most likely to be hurt or abused by a stranger. This is not true. 'Stranger danger' is a real concern, but more than half the children who call ChildLine about sexual abuse are being abused by someone in their own family. Nearly always, the abuser is someone known to the child.

Nine out of ten children who phone ChildLine about sexual abuse say they are abused by men. ChildLine also hears from children who are abused by other young people. Women are as likely as men to abuse children physically or emotionally or to neglect them.

Abusers can be rich or poor, black or white, have any job or be unemployed. They include parents, step-parents, uncles, aunts, grandparents, teachers, family friends, brothers and sisters.

### What happens when an abused child calls ChildLine?

*'A lot of children wouldn't want to talk to you face to face – they don't want to have to deal with you, your expressions, or you looking at them. They've been threatened and intimidated and told that no one will ever believe them. It means going to a counsellor and having to say, "I've been abused" feels impossible – it's easier on the phone. Children have anonymity, privacy and confidentiality. They can end the call when they like.'* ChildLine counsellor

When children call ChildLine, we don't push them to take action immediately, but try to help them at their own pace. ChildLine has learned that to do anything else can mean a child may never call again – some children are as afraid of intervention as they are of the abuse continuing.

Calling ChildLine gives children the opportunity to talk to someone 'safe', someone who will not judge them. Children often find it very difficult to talk about being abused. They sometimes feel the abuse is their fault, and they worry greatly about what will happen if they tell – either because they are afraid of getting a loved one into trouble or because they have been threatened into keeping silent, or a combination of both. In many cases, they are worried that they will be taken away from home and that their families will be broken up.

They are afraid of being taken from their home, of being made to face their abuser, or being made to tell strangers what has happened – even of an abusing parent whom they still love being sent to prison.

ChildLine puts the interests of the child first. Just by being on the end of the line our counsellors help relieve some of the loneliness and desperation that abused children feel. They help children understand that the abuse they have suffered is not their fault.

Sometimes during one call, or perhaps over many months, ChildLine counsellors talk through with a child what has happened, and what they can do. Experience has taught us that this helps children to find the confidence finally to tell a teacher, a parent or a friend – though in some situations ChildLine will intervene directly to help a child.

### Do ChildLine counsellors report abuse to the police?

Generally, if a child phones Child-Line to talk about being abused, nothing is passed on to the police or social services unless the child wants this to happen.

In some situations though, such as if a child is very young and unable to get help themselves or if a child's life is in danger, ChildLine intervenes directly to ensure the child's safety.

### What does child abuse do to children?

*'I think my dad's sexually abusing me... he hits me too. If I don't do what I'm told, he does dirty things. I feel disgusting and ashamed. I want to kill myself. I tell him to stop but he won't. I've tried to tell my mum, but I can't get the courage. It would break her heart and she might not believe me.' Rosie, 14*

While some forms of abuse can be seen – like bruises and burns – many others can't. Yet all forms of child abuse can do long-term or even permanent damage to a child's wellbeing and development. Young people who call ChildLine about their abuse often tell us they feel worthless, unloved and betrayed. They are often confused and frightened, and many feel incapable of trusting other people or unworthy of another's love. Abused children can lose confidence, become withdrawn or aggressive, and may lose the ability to concentrate.

It is not at all uncommon for a victim to suffer severe depression, which can lead to self-harm – sometimes to attempts at suicide. This loss of confidence and sense of betrayal can also make it difficult for them to develop relationships and get on at school.

Many children tell ChildLine that, while they want the abuse to stop, they are afraid of splitting up their family.

Children often feel guilty and blame themselves for the abuse. They can also feel ashamed and embarrassed. ChildLine assures children and young people that they are not to blame, and helps them to understand that talking about the problem can be a first step in improving their situation.

### How can children be protected from abuse?

There are laws to protect children and to deal with people who abuse them. The most important laws are the Children Act 1989 (England and Wales), the Children (Scotland) Act 1995 and the Children (Northern Ireland) Order 1995. These acts say what should happen if a child is being abused or is at risk of harm.

### What happens when a child tells someone they are being abused?

Childcare professionals, such as teachers, are obliged to tell the police or social services if they suspect or know about abuse. Social workers must look into reports of child abuse. First of all, a social worker may talk to the child and parents, and try to decide whether or not a child is being neglected or abused.

ChildLine believes it is essential that social workers, police officers, doctors or others looking into abuse talk to children on their own.

### How do the police and social workers investigate child abuse?

Sometimes people looking into child abuse decide to have a child protection conference. Anyone who knows the child and the family can be invited to attend. Generally this includes teachers, doctors, health visitors, play workers, and other people who know the child, as well as police and social workers. The child can suggest who they would like to attend the conference. At the conference, children and families are asked for their views. Children can always ask to speak on their own – supported by a teacher or friend – if they feel they cannot talk about what has happened in front of their parents or other adults.

After the conference, if it is decided that the child is at risk of harm, then their name can be put on the child protection register. Conferences can recommend 'schemes' to help children and families, such as having someone help out in the home or getting extra help at school. Sometimes a conference can recommend that a child should live somewhere else – with someone else in the family, for example, or with friends or foster carers – until it is safe to live at home again.

The law can make a person who has been abusing children leave the home and keep away, so that the child can stay at home safely with other members of their family.

Once a child or young person has told somebody about being abused, the police may become involved. They may ask the child to make a video about what has happened to them. The police may need this video to bring the abuser to court. The child will be supported by someone they know and trust – or by a social worker or police officer – throughout this process.

⇨ The above information is an extract from the ChildLine factsheet *Child Abuse*. Visit www.childline.org. uk for more information. ChildLine and the NSPCC joining together for children.

© *ChildLine*

# Child abuse and neglect

## The emotional effects

### What is child abuse?

All parents upset their children sometimes. Saying 'no' and managing difficult behaviour is an essential part of parenting. Tired or stressed parents can lose control and can do or say something they regret, and may even hurt the child. If this happens often enough, it can seriously harm the child. That is why abuse is defined in law. The Children Act 1989 states that abuse should be considered to have happened when someone's actions have caused a child to suffer significant harm to their health or development.

Significant harm means that someone is:

⇨ punishing a child too much
⇨ hitting or shaking a child
⇨ constantly criticising, threatening or rejecting a child
⇨ sexually interfering with or assaulting a child
⇨ not looking after a child – not giving them enough to eat, ignoring them, not playing or talking with them or not making sure that they are safe.

### Who abuses children?

Children are usually abused by someone in their immediate family circle. This can include parents, brothers or sisters, babysitters or other familiar adults. It is quite unusual for strangers to be involved.

### How can you tell if a child is being abused?

Physically abused children may be:

⇨ watchful, cautious or wary of adults
⇨ unable to play and be spontaneous
⇨ aggressive or abusive
⇨ bullying other children or being bullied themselves
⇨ unable to concentrate, under-achieving at school and avoiding activities that involve removal of clothes, e.g. sports
⇨ having temper tantrums and behaving thoughtlessly

RC
PSYCH
ROYAL COLLEGE OF
PSYCHIATRISTS

⇨ lying, stealing, truanting from school and getting into trouble with the police
⇨ finding it difficult to trust other people and make friends.

Sexually abused children may:

⇨ suddenly behave differently when the abuse starts
⇨ think badly of themselves
⇨ not look after themselves
⇨ use sexual talk or ideas in their play that you would usually see only in someone much older
⇨ withdraw into themselves or be secretive
⇨ under-achieve at school
⇨ start wetting or soiling themselves
⇨ be unable to sleep
⇨ behave in an inappropriately seductive or flirtatious way
⇨ be fearful, frightened of physical contact

⇨ become depressed and take an overdose or harm themselves
⇨ run away, become promiscuous or take to prostitution
⇨ drink too much or start using drugs
⇨ develop an eating disorder such as anorexia or bulimia.

---

**The Children Act 1989 states that abuse should be considered to have happened when someone's actions have caused a child to suffer significant harm to their health or development**

---

Emotionally abused or neglected children may:

⇨ be slow to learn to walk and talk
⇨ be very passive and unable to be spontaneous
⇨ have feeding problems and grow slowly
⇨ find it hard to develop close relationships
⇨ be over-friendly with strangers

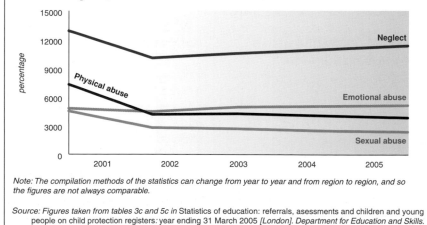

## Children on child protection registers

Children and young people on child protection registers at 31 March, by category of abuse. England, 2001-2005.

Note: The compilation methods of the statistics can change from year to year and from region to region, and so the figures are not always comparable.

Source: Figures taken from tables 3c and 5c in Statistics of education: referrals, asessments and children and young people on child protection registers: year ending 31 March 2005 [London]. Department for Education and Skills. Crown copyright.

- get on badly with other children of the same age
- be unable to play imaginatively
- think badly of themselves
- be easily distracted and do badly at school.

It can be hard to detect long-standing abuse by an adult the child is close to. It is often very difficult for the child to tell anyone about it, as the abuser may have threatened to hurt them if they tell anybody. A child may not say anything because they think it is their fault, that no one will believe them or that they will be teased or punished. The child may even love the abusing adult, they want the abuse to stop, but they don't want the adult to go to prison or for the family to break up.

If you suspect that a child is being abused, you may be able to help them to talk about it. Your local Social Services Child Protection Adviser will be able to offer more detailed advice.

### Where can I get help?
First and foremost, the child must be protected from further abuse. Social Services will need to be involved to find out:

- what has happened
- if it is likely to happen again
- what steps are needed to protect the child.

### Child protection
After investigation, Social Services may be satisfied that the problems have been sorted out, and that the parents can now care for and protect the child properly. If so, they will remain involved only if the family wants their help. If Social Services are concerned that a child is being harmed, they will arrange a child protection case conference. The parents and professionals who know the child will be invited. A plan will be made to help the child and family and ensure that there is no further harm.

### Help to look after the child
When a child has been abused within the family, the person involved is sometimes able to own up to what they have done and wants help. They can then be helped to look after their child better. Occasionally, the child may have to be taken away from the abusing adult because the risks of physical and emotional harm are too great. This can be for a short time, until things become safer, or may be permanent.

### Specialist treatment
Many children need specialist treatment because of the abuse they have endured. Some receive help from family centres run by Social Services. If they are worried, depressed or being very difficult, the child and family might need help from the local child and adolescent mental health service. These specialists may work with the whole family, or with children and adolescents alone. Sometimes they work with teenagers in groups. Individual therapy can be especially helpful for children who have been sexually abused, or who have experienced severe trauma. Children who have suffered serious abuse or neglect can be difficult to care for, and the service can offer help and advice to parents and carers.

- The above information is re-printed with kind permission from the Royal College of Psychiatrists. Visit www.rcpsych.ac.uk for more information.

*© Royal College of Psychiatrists*

# One child in ten grows up feeling unloved

### NSPCC calls on nation to Be the FULL STOP

The NSPCC today (Wednesday 13 September) launches Be the FULL STOP – a nationwide call for people to act on child cruelty. It comes as a heart-rending new survey finds one in ten adults felt unloved as children.

The study reveals the deep distress of children who are emotionally abused by their parents or carers. Of those who said they grew up feeling unloved:

- one in ten (11%) became su-icidal
- more than a quarter (28%) were depressed
- one in four (27%) were unable to concentrate in school.

The NSPCC estimates there could be 1.4 million children today who feel unloved, based on the survey findings.

Be the FULL STOP is a major new drive in the NSPCC's FULL STOP campaign to end cruelty to children. Over the next 12 months, the charity is urging at least 1.4 million people to do something to stop child cruelty – one person for every unloved child.

People can join the campaign now by phoning 08000 12 12 11 or visiting www.bethefullstop.com. There they can get on the first-ever UK map of those committed to ending child cruelty. They can see how their actions add to those of many thousands of others to make a real difference for children – through campaigning, volunteering, donating and fundraising. They will join NSPCC ambassadors like Kylie Minogue and connect with a growing community of supporters in their neighbourhood and across the country.

Unacceptable levels of emotional abuse by parents and carers were reported in the NSPCC survey. The study found:

- Seventeen per cent of children were regularly shouted or screamed at
- Six per cent were regularly really

afraid of their father, mother or carer
- ⇨ Five per cent were regularly called stupid, lazy or worthless
- ⇨ Five per cent were regularly humiliated or made to feel embarrassed
- ⇨ Four per cent were regularly hurt or upset on purpose or made to feel disliked.

The study shows how the devastating impact of missing out on a parent's love can last well into adulthood. A quarter of those unloved said it had damaged their confidence. Of this group many reported that it had left them angry and resentful (19%), damaged their adult relationships or job prospects (25%), or that it was always preying on their mind (17%).

## Five per cent were regularly called stupid, lazy or worthless

NSPCC director Mary Marsh says: 'Vast numbers of children's lives are blighted through feeling unloved. To deprive a child of love is abuse. Full Stop.

'For each child, emotional abuse is a lonely experience of suffering and misery. Being really scared of your parents, regularly being screamed at, or never being made to feel special are major causes of childhood distress.

'It doesn't have to be like this. All children should be loved, valued and able to fulfil their potential. They have a right to grow up feeling loved – without anger and hatred aimed at them. The emotional scars can last a lifetime.

'Everyone can be part of the human barrier against child abuse. People sometimes feel abuse is too big a problem for them to make a difference. Be the FULL STOP is about showing people that everything they do – however small – adds up to ending cruelty to children. Every action counts.'

The study shows how hard it is for children to escape emotional abuse. For one in three adults surveyed (33%) their ill-treatment went on throughout their childhood. For six in ten (59%), it gradually stopped only as they got older or when they left home.

To stop children and young people suffering abuse, the NSPCC is calling on the Government to fund helplines and online or text-based counselling that provide them with 24-hour access to confidential advice and support. This would mean a counsellor is always there when a child calls and that more and better services are provided to vulnerable groups such as disabled children.

Be the FULL STOP is backed by a four-week national advertising campaign on TV, billboards, press and online.
*13 September 2006*

⇨ The above information is reprinted with kind permission from the NSPCC. Visit www.nspcc.org.uk for more information.
© NSPCC

# Coming to terms with abuse

### Dealing with the abuse later in life

Sometimes victims of child abuse will block out any memory of the events or not even realise what was happening was wrong until they leave home. Going to university or getting your own flat, job and or steady relationship may suddenly bring back memories of what happened. Dealing with the emotions then can be difficult, especially if you can't remember much. You may experience some of the following:

- ⇨ Flashbacks and nightmares: You may find memories of the abuse will suddenly appear, be it during the day or in recurring nightmares.
- ⇨ Shame and guilt: You may blame yourself for the events; suffer from low self-esteem or feel too embarrassed to get help. The pressure of the memories and emotions may lead you to become severely depressed.
- ⇨ Intense anger: Often directed at the abuser, this may appear out of nowhere after you haven't seen them for a while. You may wish to confront them or completely avoid them. It may be more general.
- ⇨ Difficulty getting intimate: You may find that you avoid intimate relationships and are unable to trust other people. On the flipside you may tend to form very intense intimate relationships, which can be just as damaging.
- ⇨ Scared: You may wonder if you will ever be able to hold down a normal relationship, you may struggle to enjoy sex and you may fear becoming an abuser yourself.
- ⇨ All alone: You may feel completely isolated by the events of your past, alienated and expecting to stay that way.

### How can I deal with it?

Take care of yourself: The fact that you were abused as a child can't be changed. It was not your fault though and so try not to punish yourself. Now is the time to look after yourself, treat yourself with respect and care and try to heal. If you can't stop harming yourself, be it through starvation or cutting, seek help.

Get angry: If you are full of anger for the way you were treated in the past, try and find a way to vent these feelings. Talk to someone, either a close friend or a counsellor. It may be easier to tell a complete stranger what you are going through. Or you could keep a diary. One of the best ways to get anger out and make yourself feel more positive is through exercise.

Let yourself grieve: It may sound strange, but the experiences you had stole your childhood and you have to allow yourself to get sad about this. You need to let the feelings out and not be afraid that once you do they won't stop. By allowing them out, you should begin to feel more in control.

⇨ The above information is reprinted with kind permission from TheSite.org. Visit www.thesite.org for more information.

© TheSite.org

# Corporal punishment in schools

## Over a billion children at risk of legal beatings at school

More than 1.25 billion children – over half of the world's child population – can still legally be beaten by their teachers in school, says Save the Children.

As governments meet at the UN on 11 October to discuss whether to end violence against children, Save the Children is calling for a global ban on all violence committed against children, including at school and in the home.

### In 95 countries across the world, violence is still condoned in the classroom

The need is urgent: 97 per cent of the world's children do not have the same legal protection against violence as adults.

In 95 countries across the world, violence is still condoned in the classroom.

Corporal punishment can knock children's confidence and self-esteem, affect their ability to learn and deter children from going to school, as well as causing serious physical harm.

### Save the Children

Hussain, 14, Ethiopia, 'It was not the pain that hurt me, but the feeling of humiliation I underwent when my classmates laughed at me. That was the last day for me to be at the gate of that school.'

It is equally scandalous that 153 countries still allow corporal punishment in daycare centres and children's homes. Only 15 countries explicitly prohibit corporal punishment in the home. Over three-quarters of all children – over 1.5 billion – live in countries where such violence is legal.

Jasmine Whitbread, CEO of Save the Children UK, 'It's shocking that so many children are exposed to violence in their school where they should be learning essential life-skills. Abuse in school can wreck children's chances of getting an education, and the effects can haunt them throughout their lives. It's time the world said no to this outdated and inhumane practice.'

Save the Children's Day of Action on 19 October is uniting children across the world to demand world leaders put a stop to violence against children. Events are taking place in countries across six continents in the world's biggest child-led protest against violence.

### Only 15 countries explicitly prohibit corporal punishment in the home

Save the Children is calling for all governments to
⇨ ban all forms of violence against children wherever they occur
⇨ create an effective national child protection system
⇨ establish a child-friendly juvenile justice system
⇨ mobilise men and boys in the battle to end gender discrimination and violence against children
⇨ support the appointment of a Special Representative at the UN to drive forward the global project to end violence against children.

*5 October 2006*

⇨ The above information is reprinted with kind permission from Save the Children. Visit www.savethechildren.org.uk for more information.

*© Save the Children*

# The smacking debate

## Information from ITV

In a paper published by Family and Youth Concern in 2004, *A Reasonable Approach to Discipline*, they quoted a BMRB survey of a representative sample of 1,007 adults which found that 85 per cent agreed that 'parents should sometimes be allowed to smack their children'. Only 12 per cent agreed that, 'smacking of children by their parents should be illegal in all circumstances'. These findings are broadly similar to a survey of 2,000 adults conducted by ONS for the Department of Heath in 1998.

## In many European countries there is a ban on smacking

In that poll, 88 per cent registered their agreement that 'it is sometimes necessary to smack naughty children', with only 8 per cent disagreeing. These surveys stand in marked contrast to the results of polls conducted on behalf of the NSPCC and the Children are Unbeatable alliance, which suggest that the majority of the general public supports a change in the law on smacking.

Family and Youth Concern believe that this discrepancy is due to the way questions were asked and the language used.

Under the Children Act 2004, physical punishment, other than 'reasonable chastisement', is against the law, with a smack which leads to bruising, grazing, cuts or swellings deemed to be unacceptable. Parents who transgress face up to 5 years' imprisonment if they are convicted

The NSPCC has complained that by refusing to remove the defence of reasonable punishment from a parent smacking a child, the law has in some ways left a grey area, where children are still seen as the property of their parents. An adult slapping another adult would have no such defence open to them. In many European countries there is an outright ban on smacking. In Sweden, a ban has been in force for over 25 years.

NSPCC are also concerned that:
⇨ There is a risk that parents and children will not be treated equally. It will be hard for there to be a consistent interpretation of the law across the country.
⇨ Some children bruise more easily than others. Also, bruising shows in different ways on black children and white children.
⇨ Both these factors make the law discriminatory, in potentially offering more protection to some children than others.

Save the Children and other children's organisations also believe that all corporal punishment of children breaches fundamental human rights principles.

## More information

Smacking as a form of disciplining children has been researched and debated by many organisations. You can learn more about the arguments by visiting the following websites:

ITV is not responsible for the availability or content of any third party websites or material you access through visiting these websites.
⇨ www.families-first.org.uk – Families First is a family advocacy group, supporting the rights and responsibilities of parents to protect and guide their children and to bring them up in a reasonable manner according to their religious and philosophical convictions.
⇨ www.famyouth.org.uk – Family and Youth Concern is a national educational trust which researches the causes and consequences of family breakdown.
⇨ www.crae.org.uk – the Children's Rights Alliance for England (CRAE) is a coalition of over 370 voluntary and statutory organisations committed to the full implementation of the Convention on the Rights of the Child.
⇨ www.endcorporalpunishment.org – a Global Initiative to End All Corporal Punishment of Children.
⇨ www.prb.org.uk – the Policy Research Bureau is an independent, social policy research centre who specialise in the family and young people.
⇨ www.ccpas.co.uk – Christian Family Network CFN is a partnership of family, parenting and marriage ministries brought together by CPO www.cfnetwork.co.uk
⇨ www.savethechildren.org.uk – the UK's leading international children's charity.
⇨ www.nspcc.org.uk – UK's leading charity specialising in child protection and the prevention of cruelty to children.
⇨ www.nfpi.org – the National Family and Parenting Institute (NFPI) is an independent charity working to support parents in bringing up their children, to promote the wellbeing of families.
⇨ www.childrenscommissioner.org – Office of the Children's Commissioner for England.
⇨ www.niccy.org – Northern Ireland Commission for Children and Young People.
⇨ www.childcomwales.org.uk – Wales Commissioner for Children and Young People.
⇨ www.sccyp.org.uk – Scottish Commission for Children and Young People.
⇨ The above information is reprinted with kind permission from Gary Watts and ITV. Visit www.itv.com for more information.

*© Helen Watts for ITV, 2006*

# 'It never did me any harm...'

## Answering common defences of corporal punishment

'*Corporal punishment is a necessary part of upbringing. Children learn from a smacking or beating to respect their elders, to distinguish right from wrong, to obey rules and work hard. Without corporal punishment children will be spoilt and undisciplined.*'

---

**Children need discipline, and particularly need to learn self-discipline. But corporal punishment is a very ineffective form of discipline**

---

Children need discipline, and particularly need to learn self-discipline. But corporal punishment is a very ineffective form of discipline. Research has consistently shown that it rarely motivates children to act differently, because it does not bring an understanding of what they ought to be doing nor does it offer any kind of reward for being good. The fact that parents, teachers and others often have to repeat corporal punishment for the same misbehaviour by the same child testifies to its ineffectiveness. Smacking, spanking and beating are a poor substitute for more positive forms of discipline which, far from spoiling children, ensure that they learn to think about others and about the consequences of their actions. In the countries where corporal punishment is banned there is no evidence to show that disruption of schools or homes by unruly children has increased: the sky does not fall if children cannot be hit.

'*I was hit as a child and it didn't do me any harm. On the contrary I wouldn't be where I am today if it were not for my parents and teachers physically punishing me.*'

*Global Initiative to*
**End All Corporal Punishment of Children**

People usually hit children because they themselves were hit as children: children learn from and identify with their parents and teachers. It is pointless to blame the previous generation for hitting children because they were acting in accordance with the general culture of the time; nor should bonds of love and gratitude which children have towards their elders be denied. However times change, and social attitudes with them. There are plenty of examples of individuals who were not hit as children becoming great successes, and even more examples of individuals who were hit failing to fulfil their potential in later life.

Parents often hit out of anger and frustration – children, like adults, can be very wearisome and difficult – and because they have no knowledge of alternative methods. Parents who try alternatives report success.

'*Parents' right to bring up children as they see fit should only be challenged in extreme cases, like child abuse.*'

The UN Convention on the Rights of the Child replaces the concept of parents' rights with 'parental responsibilities' (which of course carry with them certain rights), including the responsibility to protect the rights of children themselves. The assertion of children's rights seems an unwarranted intrusion to people accustomed to thinking of children as parents' possessions, but children are now recognised as individuals who are entitled to the protection of human rights standards along with everyone else. Other forms of interpersonal violence within families – including wife-beating – are already subject to social control and are unlawful in almost every society.

'*There is a big difference between a vicious beating and the little smacks that parents often give their children. These are not dangerous, do not cause real pain and cannot be called abuse. Why should these be outlawed?*'

Firstly, the little smack does cause a child pain and is intended to do

YOU REALISE OF COURSE THAT THIS WILL HURT ME MORE THAN IT HURTS YOU!

so. And sometimes 'minor' corporal punishment causes unexpected injury. Hitting children is dangerous because children are small and fragile (much corporal punishment is targeted at babies and very young children). Ruptured eardrums, brain damage, and injuries or death from falls are the recorded consequences of 'harmless smacks'.

People would no longer get away with condemning violence to women, by defending 'little slaps'.

There is a large body of international research suggesting negative outcome from corporal punishment. The following are some of the conclusions:

⇨ **Escalation** Mild punishments in infancy are so ineffective that they tend to escalate as the child grows older. The little smack thus becomes a spanking and then a beating. Parents convicted of seriously assaulting their children often explain that the ill-treatment of their child began as physical punishment.

⇨ **Encouraging violence** Even a little slap carries the message that violence is the appropriate response to conflict or unwanted behaviour. Aggression breeds aggression. Children subjected to physical punishment have been shown to be more likely than others to be aggressive to siblings; to bully other children at school; to take part in aggressively anti-social behaviour in adolescence; to be violent to their spouses and their own children and to commit violent crimes. National commissions on violence in America, Australia, Germany, South Africa and the UK have recommended ending corporal punishment of children as an essential step towards reducing all violence in society.

⇨ **Psychological damage** Corporal punishment can be emotionally harmful to children. Research especially indicts messages confusing love with pain, anger with submission. 'I punish you for your own sake', 'I hurt you because I love you', 'You must show remorse no matter how angry or humiliated you are.' Less acknowledged are the links be-

tween corporal punishment and sexual development (reflected in much pornography, and in the common use of prostitutes for spanking and correction), and between corporal punishment and sexual abuse of children, whereby the invasion of children's physical integrity makes an easy path from one to the other.

**'I only smack my children for safety – for their own sake they must learn about danger.'**
If a child is crawling towards a hot oven, or running into a dangerous road, of course you must use physical means to protect them – grab them, pick them up, show them and tell them about the danger. But if you raise your hand to hit them, you are wasting crucial seconds and – more important – by hurting the child yourself you are confusing the message the child gets about the danger, and distracting their attention from the lesson you want them to learn.

*'Many parents in our country are bringing up their children in desperate conditions, and teachers and other staff are under stress from overcrowding and lack of resources. Forbidding corporal punishment would add to that stress and should await improvement of these conditions.'*
This argument is a tacit admission of an obvious truth: corporal punishment is often an outlet for pent-up feelings of adults rather than an

attempt to educate children. In many homes and institutions adults urgently need more resources and support, but however real adults' problems may be, venting them on children cannot be justifiable. Children's protection should not wait on improvements in the adult world, any more than protection of women from violence should have had to await improvement to men's conditions. Refraining from hurting or humiliating children does not consume or distort the deployment of resources.

In any case hitting children is an ineffective stress-reliever. Adults who hit out in temper often feel guilty; those who hit in cold blood find they have angry and resentful children to cope with. Life in homes and institutions where physical punishment has been abandoned for more positive discipline is much less stressful for all.

**'This is a white, Euro-centric issue. Corporal punishment is a part of my culture and child-rearing tradition. Attempts to outlaw it are discriminatory.'**
Historically, the hitting of children seems to be a white tradition, exported to many parts of the world through slavery and colonialism, both of which used corporal punishment as a means of control. It appears that the only cultures where children are rarely or never physically punished are small, hunter-gatherer societies, now rapidly vanishing under the impact of urbanisation – but arguably among the most 'natural' of all human cultures.

No culture can be said to 'own' corporal punishment. All cultures have a responsibility to disown it, as they have disowned other breaches of human rights which formed a part of their traditions. The UN Convention on the Rights of the Child upholds ALL children's right to protection from all forms of physical or mental violence without discrimination on grounds of race, culture, tradition or religion. There are movements to end corporal punishment of children now in all continents of the world. School and judicial beatings have been outlawed in states in all continents.

**'My religion requires the corporal punishment of children.'**

People are entitled to freedom of religion only insofar as the practice of their religion does not break the law or infringe human rights. But in fact in none of the world's great religions does the word of God require children to be beaten. Phrases such as 'spare the rod and spoil the child' do occur in some holy books, but not as a doctrinal text. Sayings which endorse peaceful solutions and kindly forms of child-rearing can be found in equal measure to punitive sayings in all religious scriptures, and in every faith there will be prominent leaders who denounce all violence to children.

**'If corporal punishment of children is outlawed or criminalised this will result in outrageous judicial or disciplinary intervention. Children will be encouraged to act like police and spies in the home.'**

In countries where corporal punishment is outlawed there have been some disciplinary actions against teachers and childcare workers who hit children. In relation to the family home, these laws are about setting standards and changing attitudes, not prosecuting parents or dividing families. Child protection becomes more straightforward once confusing legal concepts of 'reasonable chastisement' are abandoned. Research shows that parents seek help earlier when they recognise that hurting their children is socially and legally unacceptable. Welfare services recognise that children's needs are as a rule best met within their families, so provide parents with help and support rather than punitive interventions.

**'Banning physical punishment will just lead to children being treated in more horrible ways – emotional abuse, or humiliation or locking them up. How do you suggest children should be punished?'**

Children must be protected from all forms of humiliating and inhuman punishment, not only corporal punishment, and parents or staff often need guidance on alternatives

to such punishments. The starting point is not to replace one form of punishment with another, but to see discipline as a positive not punitive process, part of the communicative relationship between parent and child. Research clearly shows that effective control of children's behaviour does not depend upon punishment for wrongdoing but on clear and consistent limits that prevent it. Thereafter good discipline – which must ultimately be self-discipline – depends on adults modelling and explaining the behaviour they prefer; having high expectations of children's willingness – and realistic expectations of their developmental ability – to achieve it, and rewarding their efforts with praise, companionship and respect.

---

## Children must be protected from all forms of humiliating and inhuman punishment, not only corporal punishment

---

**'This country is a democracy but there is no democratic support for ending corporal punishment. I bet if there was a poll on the issue a huge majority would support retaining corporal punishment.'**

Representative democracies are not run by popular referenda. This means that the elected politicians will, when drawing up new laws and the constitution, make a number of unpopular decisions, based on informed arguments. Like the abolition of capital punishment, proposals to end the physical punishment of children never enjoy popular support before legal or administrative steps are taken to outlaw it. However, public attitudes rapidly change once such steps are taken.

**'I'd bet that if you asked children how they'd like to be punished they would choose corporal punishment.'**

Perhaps you could say that was a good reason not to use it! One reason some children may say they like to be physically punished is because it is 'quick'. In one sense this is true, in that a blow or a beating can quickly be shrugged off or can bring esteem from peers.

This underlines how very ineffective it is as a method of discipline.

In another sense physical punishment is not 'quick' because its hidden effects – humiliation, loss of self-esteem, encouragement of aggression and bullying – can be long-lasting. And sadly it is also true that children sometimes seek a beating as a means of gaining the attention of an adult who otherwise ignores them.

*This section is adapted from a pamphlet published by EPOCH-WORLDWIDE and Rädda Barnen – 'Hitting people is wrong – and children are people too'.*

⇨ The above information is reprinted with kind permission from the Global Initiative to End All Corporal Punishment of Children. Visit www.endcorporalpunishment.org for more information.

*© Global Initiative to End All Corporal Punishment of Children*

# A human rights issue

## Information from the Global Initiative to End All Corporal Punishment of Children

Corporal punishment of children breaches their fundamental human rights to respect for human dignity and physical integrity. Its legality in almost every state worldwide – in contrast to other forms of interpersonal violence – challenges the universal right to equal protection under the law.

The aims of the Global Initiative already have the support of UNICEF, members of the Committee on the Rights of the Child and key international human rights organisations and individuals.

In previous centuries, special defences existed in legislation in many states to justify corporal punishment of wives, servants, slaves and apprentices. Violence to women remains far too prevalent, but in most states it is no longer defended in legislation. It is paradoxical and an affront to humanity that the smallest and most vulnerable of people should have less protection from assault than adults.

During the first decade of the Convention on the Rights of the Child (CRC) its Treaty Body, the Committee on the Rights of the Child, has consistently stated that persisting legal and social acceptance of corporal punishment is incompatible with the Convention. The CRC requires states to protect children from 'all forms of physical

**Global Initiative to**
**End All Corporal Punishment**
**of Children**

and mental violence' while in the care of parents and others (article 19). The Committee has recommended that states in all continents should implement legal reforms to prohibit all corporal punishment and public education campaigns to promote positive, non-violent forms of

---

### It is paradoxical and an affront to humanity that the smallest and most vulnerable of people should have less protection from assault than adults

---

discipline, including within the family, schools and other institutions and penal systems. In particular, the Committee has condemned legal concepts which attempt to define 'acceptable' violence to children

– 'reasonable chastisement', 'lawful correction' and so on.

Just as the Committee on the Elimination of Discrimination against Women has been preoccupied with domestic violence to women, so the Committee on the Rights of the Child is now leading the challenge to violence to children. When representatives of these two Committees met in 1998 in Geneva to discuss action against family violence, they agreed that 'zero tolerance' is the only possible target. As with violence to women, the problem was recognised to be rooted in traditional attitudes and culture, sometimes underpinned by religion. But a practice which violates basic human rights cannot be said to be owned by any culture, nor dictated by any religion.

Other human rights Treaty Bodies – the Human Rights Committee, Committee on Economic, Social and Cultural Rights (in a recent General Comment) and the Committee Against Torture – have also condemned corporal punishment of children in various contexts, but not as yet comprehensively. The United Nations rules and guidelines on juvenile justice all support prohibition of corporal punishment. In 1999, a resolution of the Commission on Human Rights called on states 'to take all appropriate national, bilateral and multilateral measures to prevent all forms of violence against children...'. It requested all relevant human rights mechanisms, in particular special rapporteurs and working groups, within their mandates, 'to pay attention to the special situations of violence against children'.

There have been various landmark judgments, quoting human rights principles and condemning corporal punishment of children, from constitutional and other high-level courts at national level – for example in India, Israel, Italy, Namibia, South Africa, and Zimbabwe – and from the

European Court of Human Rights. There is a current constitutional challenge to corporal punishment in Canada.

The Global Initiative to End All Corporal Punishment of Children aims to ensure that the recommendations of the Committee on the Rights of the Child and other human rights bodies are accepted and that governments move speedily to implement legal reform and public education programmes.

Children should not have to wait any longer to enjoy the basic right to respect for their human dignity. Without co-ordinated action to disseminate information on legal reform and public education campaigns and to mobilise a range of partners, progress will be slow. Corporal punishment is in most countries a deeply embedded traditional practice and political and other leaders do not find abolition popular. It is a deeply personal issue: most people were hit as children; most parents have hit their children. We do not like to think badly of our parents or our parenting. This makes it difficult at first for many people to accept the human rights imperative for challenging and ending all corporal punishment.

### Progress towards ending corporal punishment

Despite the growing consensus that corporal punishment breaches children's fund-amental human rights, most of the world's children are still subjected to legalised assaults by their parents and by other carers and teachers.

In states in every continent there have been moves to end corporal punishment in schools and penal systems (for example, in recent years in Ethiopia, Korea, South Africa, Thailand, Trinidad and Tobago and Zimbabwe) and the issue is on the political agenda in many other states.

At least 10 countries have abolished all corporal punishment of children and more have reforms under discussion.

Instituting the necessary legal changes is not expensive: what is required in almost every state is the explicit and well-publicised removal of any defence which currently justifies physical assault of children, in order to ensure that children have equal protection under the law. Promotion of positive discipline can be built into other health promotion, education and early childhood development programmes.

### The other arguments against corporal punishment of children

The imperative for removing adults' assumed rights to hit children is that of fundamental human rights. Research into the harmful physical and psychological effects of corporal punishment, into the relative significance of links with other forms of violence, in childhood and later life, add further compelling arguments for condemning and ending the practice, suggesting that it is an essential strategy for reducing all forms of violence, in childhood and later life.

There is some danger that in becoming too preoccupied with this absorbing research, people forget the human rights imperative for action now: we do not look into the effects of physical discipline on women, or on animals. It is enough that it breaches fundamental rights. Finding some positive short- or long-term effects of corporal punishment would not reduce the human rights imperative for banning it.

Children, for too long the silent victims of corporal punishment, are beginning to express their own views about it. The Convention on the Rights of the Child requires states to enable children to express their views freely on all matters affecting them, and to give their views due consideration. Hearing children's voices should help to speed the end of corporal punishment.

⇨ The above information is reprinted with kind permission from the Global Initiative to End All Corporal Punishment of Children. Visit www.endcorporalpunishment.org for more information.

© Global Initiative to End All Corporal Punishment of Children

# Against a smacking ban

**Children's Commissioners are trespassing where they have no business in seeking to impose anti-smacking views by force of law**

In their demand for a new law making it a criminal offence for parents to smack their children, the UK's four children's commissioners are championing a radical children's rights agenda and not acting as the true champions of children, according to the Family Education Trust.

## 85-90 per cent of the general public supports the use of mild physical correction as a form of discipline

The Trust's Director, Norman Wells, commented: 'The commissioners seem to have lost all sense of proportion. There is already legislation in place to protect children from violence and ill-treatment and the vast majority of parents are well able to tell the difference between a disciplinary smack and genuine child abuse. Public opinion polls tell us that 85-90 per cent of the general public supports the use of mild physical correction as a form of discipline. If the commissioners had their way, loving parents could be subjected to social service investigations and even find themselves in court for disciplining their children in a way that hasn't caused the slightest degree of harm.'

The commissioners' statement makes reference to other European countries that have imposed laws against smacking, but omits to note that in Sweden, the first country to legislate against smacking in 1979, reported cases of child abuse increased almost fivefold between 1981-1994, and there was a 519 per cent increase in incidents of child-on-child violence between 1984-1994.

The statement further asserts that the UK is required to impose a ban on all smacking in order to fulfil its human rights obligations. However, the United Nations Convention on the Rights of the Child is silent on the issue and the European Court of Human Rights has repeatedly insisted that 'a certain level of severity' must be reached for physical punishment to fall foul of the European Convention on Human Rights.

Norman Wells noted: 'The use of a moderate disciplinary smack is perfectly consistent with respect for a child's human dignity and physical integrity. The commissioners seem to have lost sight of the fact that parents are authority figures in their children's lives, charged with the responsibility of caring for their children, nurturing them, and correcting them where necessary. As with any other authority figure, parents need to have sanctions at their disposal when their children misbehave, and they must be free to exercise their discretion and judgment with respect to their use. In seeking to dictate how parents may and may not bring up their children, the commissioners are trespassing on territory where they have no business.'

*22 January 2006*

⇨ The above information is reprinted with kind permission from the Family Education Trust. Visit www. famyouth.org.uk for more information.

© *Family Education Trust*

# Smacking ban rejected

**Government rejects calls to make smacking illegal**

A demand from the UK's child commissioners for the government to ban smacking has been turned down by the government. The decision to let parents make the final decision comes barely a week after Tony Blair admitted on TV that he had smacked his children.

The commissioners urged the government to introduce a tighter law whereby smacking would be completely banned, calling the change in law a 'fundamental principle'. But the plea was rejected by the Department of Education which said it was up to parents to decide what 'reasonable punishment' consisted of, adding: 'They have to think carefully about the law on assault and make sure that chastisement does not get to that point. If not they will be prosecuted.'

*23 January 2006*

⇨ The above information is reprinted with kind permission from Raising Kids. Visit www.raisingkids.co.uk for more information.

© *Raising Kids*

# Lawfulness of corporal punishment

## Information from the Global Initiative to End All Corporal Punishment of Children

### Home

Corporal punishment is lawful in the home, though the defence of 'reasonable chastisement' has been limited by amendments to the law in England and Wales and in Scotland. English common law has allowed parents and others who have 'lawful control or charge' of a child to use 'moderate and reasonable' chastisement or correction. A ruling in 1860 by Chief Justice Cockburn stated: 'By the law of England, a parent ... may for the purpose of correcting what is evil in the child, inflict moderate and reasonable corporal punishment, always, however, with this condition, that it is moderate and reasonable.' It was left to the courts to decide what is meant by 'moderate and reasonable' in any particular case.

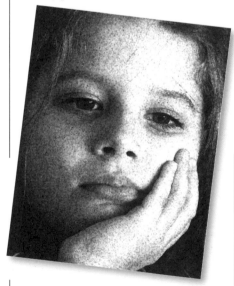

In Scotland the common law defence was restricted by a provision in the Criminal Justice (Scotland) Act (2003), section 51 of which introduces the concept of 'justifiable assault' of children, defining blows to the head, shaking and use of implements as unjustifiable. In determining whether an assault is justifiable, courts are required to consider a list of factors. In England and Wales, section 58 of the Children Act (2004, in force 2005) enables parents to justify common assault of their children as 'reasonable punishment', but prevents the defence being used in relation to more serious assault charges. In Northern Ireland, the common law defence is restricted by the Law Reform (Miscellaneous Provisions) (Northern Ireland) Order (2006) to the lowest charge of common assault and is not available for offences such as wounding, assault occasioning actual bodily harm, grievous bodily harm or cruelty to a child.

---

**Corporal punishment is lawful in the home, though the defence of 'reasonable chastisement' has been limited by amendments to the law in England, Wales and Scotland**

---

### Schools

Corporal punishment was prohibited in all state-supported education in 1986 (effective 1987). The prohibition was extended to cover private schools in England and Wales in 1998 (effective 1999), in Scotland in 2000, and in Northern Ireland in 2003.

### Penal system

Corporal punishment is unlawful as a sentence for crime and as a disciplinary measure in penal institutions.

### Alternative care

Corporal punishment is prohibited by regulation in residential care institutions throughout the UK (Children's Homes Regulation Act, 2001, and Residential Establishments Child Care (Scotland) Regulations, 1996). It is prohibited in foster care arranged by local authorities or voluntary organisations but is lawful in private foster care. In day care institutions and childminding, it is prohibited by regulations issued in 2002 for Wales and Scotland and in 2003 for England. Guidance states that physical punishment should not be used in day care institutions and childminding in Northern Ireland.

### Prevalence research

The UK Department of Health commissioned a large-scale Community Study of Physical Violence to Children in the Home and Associated Variables in the 1990s. It found very high frequency of physical punishments, including severe punishment. The large majority (91%) of children had been hit. Frequency of hitting declined with age. Only 25% of the babies aged up to one year in the study had never been smacked by their mothers; 14% of these one-year-olds had been smacked with 'moderate' severity, and 38% had been smacked more than once a week. The study included interviews with both parents in 99 two-parent families. It found that one-fifth of children in these families had been hit with an implement and over one-third (35%) had at some time experienced a punishment that was rated as 'severe' (defined as punishments 'that were intended to, had the potential to, or actually did cause physical and/or psychological injury or harm to the child'). (Nobes, G. et al., 1997, 'Physical punishment of children in two-parent families', *Clinical Child Psychology and Psychiatry*, vol. 2, no. 2, pp.271-281; also summary presented as a poster by Dr Marjorie Smith at the Fifth European Conference on Child Abuse and

Neglect, International Society for the Prevention of Child Abuse and Neglect, Oslo, May 1995)

Research by Save the Children in Scotland, carried out in 2000, looked at the opinions of 1,319 children and young people aged 6-18 years, using focus groups and questionnaires. Of the 1,249 children who completed the questionnaires, 93% said there were other ways that parents could discipline their children, without hitting them. 76% believed that it is wrong for a parent or other adult to hit a child. Most believed that hitting was the result of a parent's feelings of anger, stress and frustration, rather than a reasonable act, and most described feeling distressed when they were hit. (Cutting, E., 2001, 'It doesn't sort anything': A report on the views of children and young people about the use of physical punishment, Edinburgh: Save the Children)

Research by Save the Children in Northern Ireland, published in 2002, involved questionnaires and interviews with 189 children aged 4-11 years. Two-thirds believed that children were hit because they are 'bad, bold, cheeky, doing things wrong or doing wrong things'; one in four believed that children are hit because of how the adult is feeling. More than 80% of children used words like 'hurt, sad, sore, upset, unhappy, unloved, heartbroken, awful' to describe how they felt when they were hit. 94% said they would not smack their children when they themselves became parents. Fewer than three in 20 thought it was acceptable for an adult to hit a child. (Horgan, G., 2002, It's a hit, not a 'smack': A booklet about what children think about being hit or smacked by adults, Belfast: Save the Children)

Comparable findings were revealed in similar research by Save the Children in England and in Wales. (Crowley, A. & Vulliamy, C., Listen Up! Children Talk: About Smacking, Cardiff: Save the Children; Willow, C. & Hyder, T., 1998, It hurts you inside – children talking about smacking, National Children's Bureau and Save the Children)

In a survey for the National Society for the Prevention of Cruelty to Children in Northern Ireland and the Irish Society for the Prevention of Cruelty to Children of 1,100 children aged 8-15 years, almost a tenth of children reported that teachers threatened to slap them, and 4% said that they actually did, even though corporal punishment is banned. One-fifth said their parents smacked them, though relationships with parents were positive. (McGill, P., 1996, 'Pupils in Ireland fear test failure', Times Educational Supplement, 23 August 1996)

## Recommendations by human rights treaty bodies

### Committee on the Rights of the Child

'The Committee welcomes the abolition of corporal punishment in all schools in England, Wales and Scotland following its 1995 recommendations (ibid., para. 32) but is concerned that this abolition has not yet been extended to cover all private schools in Northern Ireland. It welcomes the adoption by the National Assembly for Wales of regulations prohibiting corporal punishment in all forms of day care, including childminding, but is very concerned that legislation prohibiting all corporal punishment in this context is not yet in place in England, Scotland or Northern Ireland.

'In light of its previous recommendation (ibid., para. 31), the Committee deeply regrets that the State party persists in retaining the defence of "reasonable chastisement" and has taken no significant action towards prohibiting all corporal punishment of children in the family.

'The Committee is of the opinion that the Government's proposals to limit rather than to remove the "reasonable chastisement" defence do not comply with the principles and provisions of the Convention and the aforementioned recommendations, particularly since they constitute a serious violation of the dignity of the child (see similar observations of the of the Committee on Economic, Social and Cultural Rights, E/C.12/1/Add.79, para. 36). Moreover, they suggest that some forms of corporal punishment are acceptable, thereby undermining educational measures to promote positive and non-violent discipline.

'The Committee recommends that the State party:
a. with urgency adopt legislation throughout the State party to remove the "reasonable chastisement" defence and prohibit all corporal punishment in the family and in any other contexts not covered by existing legislation;
b. promote positive, participatory and non-violent forms of discipline and respect for children's equal right to human dignity and physical integrity, involving children and parents and all those who work with and for them, and carry out public education programmes on the negative consequences of corporal punishment.'
(9 October 2002, CRC/C/15/Add.188, Concluding observations on second report, paras. 35, 36, 37 and 38 (a and b))

'The Committee is disturbed about the reports it has received on the physical and sexual abuse of children. In this connection, the Committee is worried about the national legal provisions dealing with reasonable chastisement within the family. The imprecise nature of the expression of reasonable chastisement as contained in these legal provisions may pave the way for it to be interpreted in a subjective and arbitrary manner. Thus, the Committee is concerned that legislative and other measures relating to the physical integrity of children do not appear to be compatible with the provisions and principles of the Convention, including those of its articles 3, 19 and 37. The Committee is equally concerned that privately funded and managed schools are still permitted to administer corporal punishment to children in attendance there which does not appear to be compatible with the provisions of the Convention, including those of its article 28, paragraph 2...

'The Committee is also of the opinion that additional efforts are required to overcome the problem of violence in society. The Committee recommends that physical punishment of children in families be prohibited in the light of the provisions set out in articles 3 and 19 of the Convention. In connection with the child's right to physical integrity, as recognised by the Convention, namely in its articles 19, 28, 29 and 37, and in the light of the best interests of the child, the Committee suggests that the State party consider the possibility of undertaking additional education campaigns. Such measures would help to change societal attitudes towards the use of physical punishment in the family and foster the acceptance of the legal prohibition of the physical punishment of children.

'... Legislative measures are recommended to prohibit the use of corporal punishment in privately funded and managed schools.'
(15 February 1995, CRC/C/15/ Add.34, Concluding observations on initial report, paras. 16, 31 and 32)

## Committee on Economic, Social and Cultural Rights

'The Committee is alarmed by the fact that corporal punishment continues to be practised in schools which are privately financed, and at the statement by the delegation that the Government does not intend to eliminate this practice.

'The Committee recommends that the State party take appropriate measures to eliminate corporal punishment in those schools in which this practice is still permitted, i.e. privately financed schools.'
(4 December 1997, CESCR/E/C.12/1/ Add.19, Concluding observations on third report, paras. 16 and 28)

## Human Rights Committee

'The Committee recommends that corporal punishment administered to privately funded pupils in independent schools be abolished.'
(27 July 1995, CCPR/C/79/Add.55, Concluding observations on fourth report, para. 8)

## European Committee of Social Rights

'The Committee recalls that Article 17 of the Charter requires a prohibition in legislation against any form of violence against children, whether at school, in other institutions, in their home or elsewhere. It furthermore considers that this prohibition must be combined with adequate sanctions in penal or civil law.

'The Committee notes that information from the report on the Regulations on Children's Homes which do not allow corporal punishment as a disciplinary measure in children's homes, in England, Wales and Scotland. It asks whether such a regulation exists for Northern Ireland.

'It notes from another source that legislation prohibiting corporal punishment in all forms of day care, including child minding, has not yet been put in place in England, Scotland or Northern Ireland. Since the precise situation is not clear, the Committee asks that the next report contain detailed information on the prohibition of corporal punishment in all child-care settings, including private ones.

'The Committee further notes from the same source that the abolition of corporal punishment in all schools in England, Wales and Scotland, has not yet been extended to cover all private schools in Northern Ireland. It asks that the next report provide more information on this.

'The Committee notes that corporal punishment within the family is not prohibited. It further notes from the abovementioned source that the defence of "reasonable chastisement" still exists and the State has taken no significant action towards prohibiting all corporal punishment of children in the family. Therefore, it considers that since there is no prohibition in legislation of all corporal punishment in the home, the situation is not in conformity with Article 17 of the Charter.

'The Committee concludes that the situation in the United Kingdom is not in conformity with Article 17 of the Charter on the grounds that: corporal punishment in the home is not prohibited...'
(July 2005, Conclusions XVII-2)

'As regards corporal punishment, the Committee notes that it was prohibited in private schools by the School Standards and Framework Act 1998, with the result that corporal punishment is now prohibited in all schools. The Committee wishes to be informed whether legislation prohibits corporal punishment in other institutions caring for children. It notes that not all forms of corporal punishment are prohibited within the family. The Committee refers to its general observations on Article 17 in the General introduction and decides to defer its conclusion on this point pending more information from the British Government on the situation and on its intentions in this regard. It also wishes to receive information on the situation in Northern Ireland and Scotland...

'Pending the information requested ... on corporal punishment, the Committee defers its conclusion.'
(1 January 2001, Conclusions XV-2 vol. 2, pages 612-617)
Updated August 2006

⇨ The above information is reprinted with kind permission from the Global Initiative to End All Corporal Punishment of Children. Visit www. endcorporalpunishment. org for more information.

# Child discipline

**As a UK-wide charity that works for, and with, parents, Parentline Plus identify the discipline of children as 'positive' or 'negative'**

'Positive discipline rests on the loving relationship between children and parents; assumes that children want to behave well; focuses on good behaviour; expects it; makes sure children understand what it is and why; rewards children for it and thus motivates them to keep on trying.

---

> ### 'Positive discipline rests on the loving relationship between children and parents'

---

'Negative discipline, on the other hand, rests on the power parents have over children; assumes that children have to be forced to behave well; focuses on bad behaviour; expects it, watches out for it, punishes children for it and hopes that will frighten them into doing the opposite.'

Parentline Plus believe that parents who adopt a consistent, positive approach to discipline tend to have to punish their children far less than those who adopt a very permissive attitude or, alternatively, those who are too authoritarian.

According to a National Parenting Institute Report (2001) Researchers have identified four key ways of parenting, each with different characteristics, and different approaches to managing children's behaviour:

⇨ authoritative (warm, firm expectations of children, encouraging children's independent thinking, with firm but moderate discipline).

⇨ authoritarian (too little warmth and respect for the child's individuality, and too much emphasis on making demands of children and firm discipline).

⇨ permissive (too little emphasis on expectations of children).

⇨ neglectful (too little warmth and involvement).

NFPI reviews of research suggest that an authoritative approach by parents produces the best outcomes for children, as it brings together both affection and firm expectations of behaviour.

Positive Parenting approaches are encouraged by most leading organisations working for children and parents. Many of them publish advice literature and other resources to help parents wishing to use alternative methods of discipline to smacking.

⇨ The above information is reprinted with kind permission from Gary Watts and ITV. Visit www.itv.com for more information.

*© Helen Watts for ITV, 2006*

## Most parents smack

**Majority in favour of smacking, but confused on legality**

One in seven parents in this country smack their children. That's the sobering results of a survey by ITV to accompany its programme *I Smack and I'm Proud* which airs this week. The results show an overwhelming support for the right of parents to discipline their children in the way they see fit. 80% of the parents believed in the right to smack – while almost three-quarters felt that any ban on smacking would lead to a deterioration in children's behaviour.

The survey also showed that parents were confused about changes to the law regarding smacking. Just 43% understood the current laws correctly – that physical chastisement was acceptable as long as it didn't leave a mark. The rest of those surveyed either believed that smacking was actually illegal, or that there were no restrictions against it.

*20 September 2006*

⇨ The above information is reprinted with kind permission from Raising Kids. Visit www.raisingkids.co.uk for more information.

*© Raising Kids*

# It hurts you inside

## Young children talk about smacking

### Children's main messages

Children spoke powerfully and eloquently. They did not only express themselves through words; they also stood up and gave graphic demonstrations of being smacked.

They had ten key messages:

1 Smacking is hitting. Most of the 76 children who took part in this study described a smack as a hard or very hard hit.
2 Smacking hurts.
3 Smacking is wrong. The vast majority of the children who took part disapproved of smacking.
4 Children react badly to being smacked. They get upset and angry and sometimes they want to smack someone else.
5 Adults regret smacking.
6 Parents and other grown-ups are the people who most often smack children.
7 Children usually get smacked indoors, and they most often get smacked on their bottom, arm or head.
8 Children do not smack adults because they are scared they will be hit again.
9 Adults do not smack each other because they are big and know better, and because they love and care about each other.
10 Half the children involved in this study said they would not smack children when they are adults. The youngest children (five-year-olds) were the most emphatic about this.

### What is a smack?

Most children (43 out of 76) described a smack as 'a hit', 'a hard hit' or 'a very hard hit'. Only one child described a smack as being a 'pat', though she quickly added 'only harder'.

'[It's] when someone hits you really hard.' (five-year-old girl)
Child (aged six): It's a really hard hit.
Adult: Can it be a soft hit?
Child: No.
'A smack is when people hit you and it

### Most children (43 out of 76) described a smack as 'a hit'

stings and I cry.' (five-year-old girl)
'It's like very hard hitting and it hurts you.' (six-year-old girl)
'It's when someone is cross with you, they hit you and it hurts.' (seven-year-old girl)

Children frequently stood up to give a demonstration of smacking. They swung their hands towards their legs, bottom and arms to hit themselves with different degrees of force. On some occasions, they gave a demonstration but then explained that a 'real smack' would be a lot harder. A seven-year-old girl observed:

'[A smack is] parents trying to hit you, [but] instead of calling [it] a hit they call it a smack.'

### What does it feel like to be smacked?

This question was answered in two ways. First, children described the physical sensations of being smacked; second, they talked about how smacking makes them feel inside.

The overwhelming message is that smacking hurts, physically and emotionally. Many children vividly described the physical pain inflicted by smacking:

'It feels like someone banged you with a hammer.' (five-year-old girl)

'It hurts and it's painful inside – it's like breaking your bones.' (seven-year-old girl)
'It's like when you're in the sky and you're falling to the ground and you just hurt yourself.' (seven-year-old boy)
'[It feels] like someone's punched you or kicked you or something.' (six-year-old boy)

The emotional impact was clear too:

'[It] hurts your feelings inside.' (seven-year-old girl)
'[It makes you] grumpy and sad and also really upset inside. And really hurt.' (five-year-old girl)
'It hurts a lot, it makes you unhappy.' (six-year-old girl)
'You cry and you're miserable.' (five-year-old boy)
'You're hurt and it makes you cry [and] drips come out of your eyes.' (five-year-old girl)

Children explained how smacking can have a negative effect on parent-child relationships:

'And you feel you don't like your parents anymore.' (seven-year-old girl)
'It feels, you feel sort of as though you want to run away because they're sort of like being mean to you and it hurts a lot.' (seven-year-old girl)

Asking for help does not always work. A five-year-old girl explained:

'It feels bad or sad when your dad or mum smacks you – you try and tell your aunties but they do nothing.'

Some children described feeling embarrassed and ashamed:

## Will you smack when you are big?

Percentage of children surveyed who said they will not smack children when they are big.

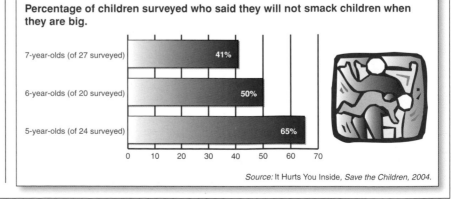

| | |
|---|---|
| 7-year-olds (of 27 surveyed) | 41% |
| 6-year-olds (of 20 surveyed) | 50% |
| 5-year-olds (of 24 surveyed) | 65% |

*Source:* It Hurts You Inside, *Save the Children, 2004.*

'It feels like [they] shouldn't have done that, it hurts. It feels embarrassed, it feels like you are really sorry and it hurts.' (seven-year-old girl)

## Who usually smacks children?

All of the children who answered this question mentioned parents. Mums were mentioned slightly more than dads. Most of the children (52 out of 76) mentioned grandparents. A six-year-old girl explained:
'Well, I think mostly family and sometimes friends who get quite cross with you like [your] mum and dad, grandma and grandad and friends that live quite near here, in the same street.'

---

**Smacking is hitting. Most of the 76 children who took part in this study described a smack as a hard or very hard hit**

---

A five-year-old girl gave the following list:
'Their parents or your mummy or your daddy or your grandad or your auntie or your grandma or people in your house – a big person has to hit a little person because they're naughty.'
A seven-year-old girl said:
'Let's say your mum and dad have gone out and you've been naughty, your grandmother [will smack you but] mostly your mum and dad.'
Aunts and uncles were specifically mentioned and some children mentioned adults who are not relatives, including nannies (those paid to look after children in the home).
A six-year-old girl listed 'mums and dads and aunties and foster people and foster children'.
A seven-year-old girl said, 'Usually their parents and relations and occasionally you might get a teacher' while a five-year-old said, 'sometimes babysitters'.
Strangers also presented potential dangers to children.
A five-year-old boy listed 'thieves, kidnappers, mums and dads [and] nasty men' as people that usually smack children. A five-year-old girl described lots of adults being around when a child is being hit:
'Sometimes your uncles and aunties are there and your mum and dads are there and they can smack you really hard or they can smack you with a cane.'

## Where do children usually get smacked?

It was assumed by the researchers that children would begin by talking about where on the body children are usually smacked, but almost all of them talked immediately about the location in which children are smacked. Children's statements were revealing:
'[Children get smacked] in a corner because the parents wouldn't want to do it so everyone could see 'cos then [the children] might call someone else and they might come and take the children, so they'll go in a corner and smack.' (six-year-old boy)
A seven-year-old boy said:
'If there were thousands of people looking, then [the] mum as well as the child will get very embarrassed probably … it would be a bit rude to do it in front of everybody.'
Some children said that parents are not inhibited in public spaces:
'It depends where … you've done it, because sometimes if you were naughty in the street, [the mum] would usually just do it straight away, otherwise they would do it again. So I think wherever you did it, even if there is anyone looking.' (seven-year-old boy)
'When you go shopping and take something and you go and ask your parents and your parents will hit you and embarrass you.' (five-year-old girl)
Most children (53 out of 76) said that children are smacked in the home (the bedroom was the most common place). Shopping was the next most common location, followed by the house of a grandparent or other relative.
In terms of where on their bodies children are smacked, children said it is usually on the bottom. But being smacked on other parts of the body was also common:
'On my bum, on my face, on my head and on my arm and on the belly and on the legs.' (five-year-old girl)
'I think children usually get smacked on the side of their face or on their tummy.

Sometimes it depends how they were. If they were really naughty, it would be on their bottom but sometimes it's usually on their hands.' (seven-year-old)
'[They] hit you on the head where they're not supposed to hit you.' (seven-year-old boy)

## Will you smack children when you are big?

The younger children were significantly less in favour of smacking than the older children. This may be related to children's experience of being hit (research shows that parental physical punishment is more prevalent among toddlers and younger children), or it could be that older children have started to rationalise and take on the prevalent adult attitude that smacking is a legitimate part of parenting.

A six-year-old boy said:
'I would smack children when I'm at the age of 20 or an adult because if I'm a parent you have to smack children.'
Another six-year-old boy advised:
'No, cos it's nasty and you go in a huff, and they hit you.'
There was considerable concern among children about the effects of parents smacking children, children then smacking their own children, and the 'habit' continuing into future generations.
'No, because I think smacking is not very nice and I when I grow up I hope my children will be nice. And I'm not gonna smack them because … say when they grow up and they can still remember that day when they got smacked … and then they'll start a fight … and they'll smack little children.' (seven-year-old boy)
'Because it's mean and it hurts the child and they'll just learn to smack people and they'll go on and it won't help at all.' (seven-year-old girl)

Children who said they would not smack when they are adults said they wanted to have positive relationships with children. A five-year-old girl explained:

*'Because I'm going to make friends with the little child and I'm going to take them to the park or a party or a disco.'*

Another five-year-old said he wouldn't smack because *'I want to be friendly'*.

### Is it wrong to smack?

Almost all the children who answered this question (66 out of 72) said smacking is wrong. Many referred to smacking generally rather than thinking about whether it is wrong just for adults to smack children.

The answers to this question once again revealed the physical and emotional pain inflicted by smacking:

*'It's painful and it sets a wrong example for other people.'* (seven-year-old girl)

*'It hurts and you could break a bone or something. If you did it hard enough, you could damage something.'* (seven-year-old girl)

*'When you're smacked, you might have a very big cut and you might feel very poorly and you might have a stomach ache and they might smack your stomach and it might feel even worse.'* (seven-year-old girl)

*'It will give you a pain. It might stop your blood for a few minutes.'* (seven-year-old girl)

*'I think it's wrong because you might get hurt and you might get a bruise or a lump. And it's horrible.'* (seven-year-old girl)

The dangers in smacking were also empasised:

*'Wrong, because you might fall.'* (six-year-old boy)

A seven-year-old girl described the injustice of children being smacked for doing something accidentally:

*'Probably you did it by accident and it looked like you did it on purpose and they smacked you and it was wrong to smack.'*

### How can we stop children being smacked?

Most children interpreted this question as meaning what they or their parents could do to stop smacking. They were not asked about changing the law, although some did mention this.

Mostly children began by talking about their own behaviour; there was much emphasis on the need for children to be good.

*'Being good and do what you're told to do.'* (six-year-old boy)

*'By being good for all your life.'* (seven-year-old girl)

*'Stop being cheeky to your mam and stop telling lies and don't cause trouble with the other kids because then your mam will tell the other mam and they'll have an argument and you will cause an argument and if I tell lies I get a hiding and a smack.'* (five-year-old girl)

Children were not viewed as the sole people responsible for ending smacking; many children said that parents could act differently. Suggestions included parents sending children to their room; verbally instructing children to stop what they are doing; and encouraging children to behave positively through rewards.

Children in one group believed strongly that if parents understood what it feels like to be smacked, then they would stop. Three seven-year-old girls suggested:

*'They might have been smacked when they were little, they were brought up with smacking them so they think it's right to smack.'*

*'They might remember being smacked but not really remember how it feels because it seems so long ago. And as they got older when they thought about it they forgot how it feels.'*

*'We could tell them how it feels and if we do something naughty then they could make you stop it by telling them in words.'*

Other children gave the following advice:

*'... you can say "well, how would you feel if somebody bigger came up to you and smacked you?" And say things like that and [say], "it doesn't help at all because you're just going to make it worse".'* (seven-year-old girl)

*'If it is against the law and if people who are in special organisations [could] link to have the right to say ... put posters up in places saying ... "Please can you stop smacking children".'* (seven-year-old girl)

*'I was just thinking that if they changed the law then a lot of people will realise what they had done to their child and they would probably ... be happy that the law was changed. If they don't change the law they will think "oh well, the child doesn't mind so we can keep on doing it". But if they realise that children have been talking to adults about it then I think they will definitely realise that it hurts their child and they will be very upset with themselves.'* (seven-year-old girl)

*'If there were only six [people who believe smacking is wrong] – but I don't think there is – then I don't think he [Tony Blair] would change the law. If there is a lot of people like, I don't know, 70 or something then I think he would definitely change the law.'* (seven-year-old girl)

### What next?

All of the children in this study had something to say about smacking and it was clear that most of them were speaking from personal experience. Many gave moving accounts of what smacking feels like and why it should be stopped.

Will another generation of children grow up with similar experiences? It is up to all of us ... it is up to you.

⇨ The above information is an extract from the NCB and Save the Children publication *It Hurts You Inside* and is reprinted with permission. Visit www.ncb.org.uk for more information or to view the full document.
© Save the Children/NCB

# Abuse

### Info for young people

### What is sexual abuse?

⇨ Sexual abuse can include different kinds of activities such as:

⇨ Some types of kissing

⇨ Touching private parts of the body

⇨ Rape (being forced to have sex when you don't want to)

⇨ Being made to look at pornographic videos or magazines

⇨ Other acts which are felt by the child or young person to be abusive.

This is not the kind of sex play which is a normal part of growing up, when children and young people want to find out about each other's bodies, or when people start going out with each other.

Sexual abusers are usually stronger or in a position of power or authority over the child or young person. They use this power to get the person to take part in sexual activities.

The law tries to protect the safety and rights of children and young people. When someone sexually abuses a child or young person they are breaking the law.

### Who sexually abuses children?

Abusers are not usually strangers. Most often, they are a relative, friend of the family, neighbour, a lodger, babysitter, someone at school, or even a group. Sometimes they can be other young people – a brother or sister or one of their friends. They often secretly abuse more than one child. Sexual abuse is usually carried out by men but sometimes women do it too.

### How someone who has been abused might feel

Dirty; ashamed; depressed; worthless; frightened; worried about abusing others; confused; isolated; suicidal; angry; embarrassed; worried about sexuality; anxious; like running away; scared about having a boyfriend or girlfriend; guilty; lonely.

Being abused leads to feelings which are hard to cope with, such as feeling:

*'When I told him not to do it he said "Don't be silly, it's just a game, what do you mean you don't like it?". I felt really mixed up. Sometimes he would say "I'm doing this because I love you…it's our special secret ok?" I thought maybe it was just me. Maybe I just had the wrong feelings. Maybe all dads are like that and it's just me who's weird.'*

The person carrying out the abuse may be someone who seems to be very nice in lots of ways. This can make it very hard to accept that they are capable of sexual abuse.

*'I know this sounds really stupid now. But I thought that someone who abused people was horrible ALL the time. I didn't think they were nice too, like helping you with your homework or buying you new clothes, normal stuff, so it took a while for the penny to drop.'*

Some abusers choose to believe that there is nothing wrong in what they are doing. They may claim that those they abuse encourage them. This can cause people who are being abused a lot of confusing feelings, such as that they are to blame if they didn't tell the abuser not to do it, or if they didn't tell anyone. Many abusers rely on the age, inexperience and fear of people they abuse to be able to carry on with it.

---

**Abusers are not usually strangers. Most often, they are a relative, friend of the family, neighbour, a lodger, babysitter, someone at school, or even a group**

---

*'It all started after Dad died. I bottled up my feelings inside because Mum was really gutted. She had to work more shifts to earn enough money. Her brother looked after us in the evenings. That's when it started. He said if I told Mum, she would probably crack up because she's been through so much already.'*

Adults are responsible for looking after and protecting children and young people. Children are not responsible for protecting adults.

## How abuse can affect behaviour

Sexual abuse can also lead to other problems: not taking care of yourself; bed-wetting; difficulty sleeping; bad dreams; running away; blanking out the memory; not being able to make friends; losing your temper; eating problems; self-harming; poor concentration; using alcohol or drugs.

---

**The person carrying out the abuse may be someone who seems to be very nice in lots of ways. This can make it very hard to accept that they are capable of sexual abuse**

---

'Before I told anyone, I was scared to go to sleep at night. Even though I tried not to think about what happened, I still had nightmares. I was too tired to bother with school and just wandered around on my own. I felt like an alien, the only one in the world like this, and I couldn't tell anyone.

'Everything built up inside. I got into trouble for not doing my work, and ended up chucking a chair at someone. I was told I would be excluded if it happened again. Mum couldn't have coped with that. So I started cutting myself instead.'

People often do their best to cope with painful feelings by trying to forget about them. But this doesn't always work.

'I didn't know what to do, because I knew I'd always have to go home and face it. I thought if I could try not to think about it, squash it out of my mind it could be like it wasn't really happening. But stupid little things would remind me, make me feel horrible inside. My friends drifted away, and I started going round with people who were in trouble. We would walk out of school after registration, go shoplifting, get

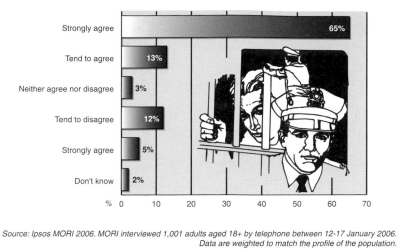

## Sentencing for child sex offenders

How much do you agree or disagree with the following statement? 'People who are imprisoned for committing serious sexual crimes against children should never be set free.'

| | |
|---|---|
| Strongly agree | 65% |
| Tend to agree | 13% |
| Neither agree nor disagree | 3% |
| Tend to disagree | 12% |
| Strongly agree | 5% |
| Don't know | 2% |

% 0 10 20 30 40 50 60 70

*Source: Ipsos MORI 2006. MORI interviewed 1,001 adults aged 18+ by telephone between 12-17 January 2006. Data are weighted to match the profile of the population.*

drunk and play chicken. Why did I do it? Because for that moment, when I was taking a risk, I knew I wouldn't be thinking about home.'

Some people feel that the only way to manage what is happening is to run away from home. If this happens, they are in a lot of danger from people who will take advantage of them. It is easy to become involved in crime or prostitution. If you are feeling like this it is VERY IMPORTANT that you get help.

## Telling someone else about sexual abuse

There are three important reasons why it's very important to get help:
⇨ Stopping the abuse
⇨ Starting to get over what happened
⇨ Protecting other children and young people.

'I didn't tell anyone about what was going on for about two years. I sort of tried to before that, by dropping hints. I tried telling someone at school by saying "If someone I knew was being abused and I told you, what would happen?" They said they'd have to tell Social Services. No way could I tell – I didn't want my family to break up and it be my fault. In the end I said something, but only because I thought he had started on my cousin.'

Telling someone about abuse may be very hard and can feel scary. You may be worried about what will happen if you talk about it, or if anyone will believe you (if they don't, don't give up, try someone else).

Sometimes it can help if you write down what you want to say first. If telling someone you know feels too difficult to begin with, you could try ringing a helpline. They can give very useful advice about any worries you might have (see national organisations).

You don't have to say who you are if you don't want to, and can say as little or as much as you want.

---

**'Loads of times I thought about taking it back, saying it was all lies. I didn't want to believe it myself. I just wanted my family back to normal'**

---

This may be the first step in helping you think about who else can support you. This could be a:
⇨ youth worker
⇨ relative
⇨ doctor
⇨ police officer
⇨ school nurse
⇨ teacher
⇨ friend
⇨ counsellor
⇨ social worker.

'When I got through to ChildLine it took a bit of time for me to say anything. They didn't hang up though. Anyway, what was really good was they couldn't see my face so they wouldn't know me if they saw me in the street. They were really patient and helped me say what I wanted in my own time, and helped me decide what to do next. When Social Services and the Police got involved they were still there for me when it felt like no one else was.'

You may find that the person that you decide to talk to will want to report the abuse to a social worker who can take steps to see that it stops. They will usually talk with you about this first.

---

**For some people it can be very useful to talk to someone trained in understanding how it feels to have been abused, and how to help**

---

If you have been abused, or someone else thinks you have been, there will be an investigation. This is when people such as a social worker, doctor or police officer try to find out what has happened, so it can be decided what should be done to help and protect you. If you have been in touch with any other agencies, they may be contacted too.

Some people worry that if they have been in trouble with the police before they will also be punished for being abused, but this is not the case. This can be an upsetting time, but remember there are people who can help you through it.

Whatever happens, even if the abuser is taken to court and is convicted, you are not responsible for what happens.

### Getting help with how you feel

Telling someone about abuse will not necessarily take away upsetting feelings. There may be times when it might seem better not to have told anyone.

'Loads of times I thought about taking it back, saying it was all lies. I didn't want to believe it myself. I just wanted my family back to normal. I just thought it would be easier to pretend it hadn't happened.'

For some people it can be very useful to talk to someone trained in understanding how it feels to have been abused, and how to help. This could be a psychotherapist, psychologist, psychiatrist or counsellor. This does not mean you are mad.

You may want to talk about what has happened to you on your own, or in a group with other young people with similar experiences. Sometimes families find it helpful to talk to a professional together. The kind of therapy offered will depend on what

is needed – and wanted.

'It helped being in a group. You know it happens to other people too, but you think you're the only one that feels the way you do. You feel less weird when you find out you're not. It helped me realise it shouldn't be me that feels ashamed, it should be him. You can see it's not other people's fault it happened to them, and they help you see it's not your fault either.'

Telling someone about abuse will not necessarily take away upsetting feelings. There may be times when it might seem better not to have told anyone.

### How can therapy help?

Young people who have decided to have some kind of therapy or counselling say that they feel much more positive about life as a result. They feel less depressed and worried, better about themselves and more able to do normal things such as schoolwork.

'Well, they didn't run out of the room in horror when I said about what happened. I wasn't sure how to handle it, so I was talking about it in a jokey way. They looked a bit serious, no sense of humour I thought. In the end it helped though, them being serious helped me take it seriously, and then take what I felt about me seriously. It helped me sort out how I felt and it wasn't so much part of my life. I could manage better at school, and could begin to get on with my life more.'

⇨ The above information is reprinted with kind permission from Young Minds. For more information, visit www.youngminds.org.uk

© Young Minds

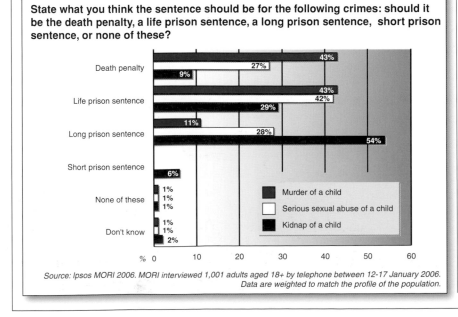

## Sentencing for crimes against children

**State what you think the sentence should be for the following crimes: should it be the death penalty, a life prison sentence, a long prison sentence, short prison sentence, or none of these?**

| | Murder of a child | Serious sexual abuse of a child | Kidnap of a child |
|---|---|---|---|
| Death penalty | 43% | 27% | 9% |
| Life prison sentence | 43% | 42% | 29% |
| Long prison sentence | 11% | 28% | 54% |
| Short prison sentence | | | 6% |
| None of these | 1% | 1% | 1% |
| Don't know | 1% | 1% | 2% |

*Source: Ipsos MORI 2006. MORI interviewed 1,001 adults aged 18+ by telephone between 12-17 January 2006. Data are weighted to match the profile of the population.*

# Child sexual abuse

## Common misunderstandings

**'Children often fantasise or make up stories about being abused – they have very active imaginations'**

This is a very old idea, and in some countries it was enshrined in law through a warning that it was not safe to convict a man on the uncorroborated evidence of a child. In fact it is extremely rare for children to lie or 'make up' stories about being sexually abused. The far bigger problem is that children are often too frightened to tell anyone.

**'Most child abusers are "paedophiles"'**

Although there are sexual abuse rings and individual abusers who target large numbers of children, most children are abused by men they know. Most child sex offenders are married men, who have sex with their wives and sometimes other adult women – they are children's fathers, uncles, teachers as well as family friends and neighbours. These men do not fit the clinical definition of 'paedophile' – adults whose sexual interest is limited to children – nor do they fit most people's perceptions of a 'paedophile' – a loner, someone with poor social skills. So most child sexual abusers are not 'paedophiles' in any clear or obvious sense.

Many people want to be able to identify a category of men who are more likely to abuse children. In fact, there is no 'type' of man who is an abuser – they come from every class, professional, racial and religious background. They are heterosexual and homosexual. They are also often very skilled at manipulating people and situations, at creating trust and respect within their community and profession, for example as clergy or youth workers.

For further discussion see: Liz Kelly, 'Weasel words: paedophiles and the cycle of abuse'.

**'Children are more likely to be abused within working-class or ethnic minority families'**

Just as there is no typical man who is

an abuser, there is no typical family where abuse takes place. Evidence from child and adult survivors reveals that sexual abuse takes place in families from all sections of society, regardless of class, race or culture. One of the reasons this idea has continued for a long time is that disadvantaged groups are those which are most likely to come under the surveillance of welfare workers and police – thus child sexual abuse is more likely to be detected in these families.

---

**There is no 'type' of man who is an abuser – they come from every class, professional, racial and religious background**

---

**'If you have been sexually abused you are likely to abuse children as an adult'**

This is a commonly held view, often referred to as 'the cycle of abuse'. If it were so simple then the majority

of child abusers should be female, since more girls than boys are sexually abused as children. But the total reverse is the case – the vast majority of child abusers are male. Some sexual abusers were abused as children, but many were not. And many children who have been abused – girls and boys – are clear that they would never treat another child that way.

This idea is popular because it is simple, and means we do not have to ask more complicated questions about power relations between adults and children, between male and female and within families.

For further discussion see: Liz Kelly, 'Weasel words: paedophiles and the cycle of abuse'.

**'Some children are very knowing and precocious beyond their years – like "Lolita" they can seduce men'**

Sometimes offenders and those defending them will argue that it was the child who initiated intimate contact, and judges have been known to make comments about 'little Lolitas'. One judge commented about a six-year-old that 'she's no angel'. It is interesting that this idea only applies to girls, no one talks about boys being 'Lolitas'.

In fact, the harmful effects of adults having sex with children have been long documented. Far from wanting or enjoying it, children are left feeling betrayed, terrified and

traumatised. The impacts go on long into adulthood. However much a child loves or cares about the adult involved, and wishes to please them, the abuse still has a devastating effect on the child's emotional well-being. Some small children having been 'sexualised' through abuse do display this kind of behaviour in their play and in their interactions with others, but this is a consequence of abuse not its cause. Adults, especially those who have caring responsibilities, have a duty to set and maintain appropriate boundaries with children, and any transgression of these boundaries is always the adult's responsibility.

---

## The most commonly reported age for child sexual abuse to start is between the ages of 4 and 6

---

Another common misunderstanding is that men, watching adolescent girls 'blossoming' into womanhood, simply cannot control themselves – particularly when the girls dress up in make-up and fashionable clothes, so they look older than they are. In fact, most child sexual abuse happens long before girls reach puberty and many survivors report abuse going back to when they have their first memories,

age 2 or 3. Babies and infants are also sexually abused. The most commonly reported age for child sexual abuse to start is between the ages of 4 and 6. This, however, does not excuse men who choose to have sex with young adolescents.

### 'Men who abuse their own children are very different from men who abuse outside the family'

This idea comes from two sources: a view in social work and psychology that incest was not about child abuse, but a way of dealing with problems in the family, usually between the adults; and early work on sex offenders which saw most sex offenders as 'sexual deviants' but excluded 'family men' from this category.

Both sets of ideas have been challenged by recent research on sex offenders. Men who abuse their own children have admitted to also abusing children outside the family and they have admitted to manipulating relationships in the family in order to facilitate their ability to abuse the child undetected. They – just like offenders outside the family do – 'groom' the child and the environment.

One of the consequences of these ideas has been that mothers in families where incest has occurred are often seen as 'collusive', and as partly to blame. Recent research in Australia revealed that abusive fathers often deliberately deceive the child, making them believe that their mother knew when she did not (Lynch, 1999).

### 'Incest should not be treated as a criminal matter – it breaks up the family and children feel responsible'

Raping and sexually assaulting children are criminal offences. Incest has historically been hidden behind closed doors and regarded as the family's 'own business'. Sometimes, authorities have worked to keep the family together rather than prosecuting the perpetrator. This has enabled perpetrators to continue to offend both within and outside the family. Such men often go on to abuse grandchildren if there are no sanctions against them.

Many children when they finally tell are angry and want justice. Others are fearful of legal processes and their father going to prison – but this invariably turns out to be the result of the abuser warning them that this will happen if they tell.

Children suffer most if abuse continues and they are not protected. They also are further hurt if they are blamed or held responsible for the split in the family. Children are best helped when the authorities take the decision to prosecute out of their hands and make it clear that adults are responsible for sorting out the situation and keeping children safe.

⇨ The above information is reprinted with kind permission from the Child and Woman Abuse Studies Unit. Visit www.cwasu.org for more information.

© London Metropolitan University

### Prison sentences for child sex abusers

Respondents were asked: 'What do you think is the appropriate prison sentence for someone found guilty of child sex abuse?'

| | percentage |
|---|---|
| Up to 5 years | 1% |
| Between 5 to 10 years | 4% |
| Between 10 to 15 years | 20% |
| They should be imprisoned for life | 60% |
| The victim's family should decide | 6% |
| They should be given some other type of sentence | 4% |
| Don't know | 5% |

Sample size: 2,310. Fieldwork: 14-16 June 2006.

Source: YouGov 2006 (www.yougov.com)

# Education on sexual abuse

## Schools fail to teach children about sexual abuse, finds NSPCC

Incomplete sex education in schools is leaving children confused about sexual abuse according to an NSPCC survey launched today, Monday June 5.

Nearly 2000 young people took part in the survey hosted on new NSPCC website donthideit.com and mykindaplace.com. Nearly all respondents (93 per cent) reported that their sex education lessons did not include any information about sexual abuse. The survey also showed that children were confused about what is illegal or wrong.

## Eighty per cent did not consider a 16-year-old having a sexual relationship with their teacher as an abusive situation

⇨ Eighty-two per cent did not realise it is illegal for a 30-year-old man to sexually touch a 15-year-old girl.

⇨ Although nearly everyone questioned (92 per cent) knew the age of consent, 88 per cent did not consider a 23-year-old woman having a sexual relationship with a 15-year-old as an abusive situation.

⇨ Eighty per cent did not consider a 16-year-old having a sexual relationship with their teacher as an abusive situation.

## 93 per cent reported that their sex education lessons did not include any information about sexual abuse

To help young people understand more about sexual abuse, the NSPCC is sending school pupils an information card about it. The pocket-sized card contains vital information about what sexual abuse is and where young people can turn if they need help or want advice.

NSPCC head of child protection awareness Chris Cloke said: 'Sex is a minefield for young people. They face a daily barrage of conflicting messages about sex and yet they don't have the knowledge to guide them through it.

'We must arm young people with a clear knowledge of where the law stands on sex and what constitutes sexual abuse. That way children will have more confidence to speak out on abuse. Three-quarters of children who have been sexually abused do not speak out about it at the time.'

The survey and the information card are the latest elements of Don't hide it, the NSPCC's drive to encourage young people to speak out on all forms of sex abuse. As part of the initiative, the NSPCC is calling on the government to improve sex education in schools. Currently, schools only have to teach the biology of sex. The NSPCC wants 14-16-year-olds in particular to be taught about sex in the context of relationships, peer pressure and the law.

Chris Cloke continued: 'Young people can't properly protect themselves from abuse or make informed decisions about sex without all the facts. That means discussing topics like emotions and relationships and what it means to be pressurised into having sex.

'We can't be coy when it comes to talking to young people about sex and sexual abuse. Young people must know that abuse is wrong no matter whoever does it.'

Also part of the Don't Hide It initiative are two 'Speak Out' Sundays to be held on 11 and 18 June. The NSPCC will be encouraging young people to speak out through a new NSPCC website www.donthideit.com.

Young people will be able to share their thoughts and feelings on the site through scenarios, polls and surveys. Discussions will be moderated by a professional social worker who will appear on the site as a virtual character.

There, they can find a confidential and anonymous space to learn what sex abuse is and how to stop it.
5 June 2006

⇨ The above information is reprinted with kind permission from the NSPCC. Visit www.nspcc.org.uk for more information.

© NSPCC

# Getting over sexual abuse

**Can you ever move on with your life after you have been abused? It is possible – here one survivor tells their story**

I was abused by my grandmother, sexually and emotionally, from pre-school until my teenage years. I was put into care for a year and abused there as well. I've come through three suicide attempts.

I started to get my life together after I left school and began to live independently. I think of myself as a survivor not a victim. I'm not pretending everything's wonderful but I have a good, enjoyable life now. I hope this will be of help to those of you going through this trauma.

---

**You may have been told no one will believe you. Keep talking until you are listened to and you are given the support you need**

---

You need somebody you can talk to, that you can trust – is there a friend or a teacher or a relative? If you don't feel happy with this phone an incest survivors' line. If you're over sixteen try to get out of the situation as soon as possible, is there someone you could stay with?

You may have been told no one will believe you. Keep talking until you are listened to and you are given the support you need. Get independent help. Getting the abuser stopped is not your responsibility, you don't need to take this on.

## Dealing with it

Your basic needs must be met before you can start to deal with the feelings. You'll need to talk about what happened and express what you've been through. You may have been holding back feelings for years: you may feel a lot or you may feel numb.

I've felt both extremes at times. Sorting through feelings that have been stuffed down for years is going to hurt and be confusing but it's worth it to have control over your life. It's alright to feel what you are feeling despite what you may have been told. You are not shameful or evil, you didn't deserve what happened. The person who told you that is the sick one not you.

## Anger

It must be expressed. I was classed as a delinquent with no prospects because I was going off all the time. I know how angry you are but listen, try to get out of the courts and the police's way, it's a long road that doesn't lead anywhere good.

You don't want any more labels hanging around your neck and you need your freedom. You're going to need time to yourself so you can let anger out in a controlled environment. Check out Martial Arts, find a club that builds confidence and strength, that gives you power back. Weight training and yoga help me not take it out on the people I care about.

## Flashbacks

This is normal; you've been through a trauma, you need to work it through, the things that helped me were writing, drawing, screaming when I felt like it. Write everything down, find somewhere safe and private to put the writing, even if you have to bury it outside.

I'm serious, you've had your privacy violated enough already. This is the time to get back your boundaries. The most 'shameful' thoughts and feelings are the ones that need to come out most. Don't feel guilty about what you think or feel.

## Depression

Let yourself cry. Again find a private place to let go. If you feel suicidal contact one of the organisations. Get a counsellor who's been through it and come out the other side. You deserve it. You need somebody who will listen and that you can trust.

Be aware of leaving yourself vulnerable if you are taking drugs of any sort. The same goes for sex. If you're having sex for cash, get your health checked at a clinic. A youth centre should be able to advise you on this. In every way stay as safe as you can be.

⇨ The above information is reprinted with kind permission from TheSite.org. Visit www.thesite.org for more information.

© TheSite.org

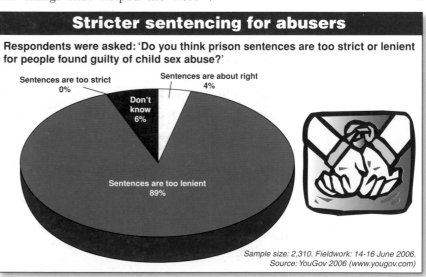

**Stricter sentencing for abusers**

Respondents were asked: 'Do you think prison sentences are too strict or lenient for people found guilty of child sex abuse?'

Sentences are too strict 0%

Sentences are about right 4%

Don't know 6%

Sentences are too lenient 89%

Sample size: 2,310. Fieldwork: 14-16 June 2006.
Source: YouGov 2006 (www.yougov.com)

# Child's play?

## Preventing abuse among children and young people

### Do children sexually abuse other children?

We are becoming increasingly aware of the risk of sexual abuse that some adults present to our children and there is growing understanding that this risk lies mostly within families and communities. But very few people realise that other children can sometimes present a risk. A third of those who have sexually abused a child are themselves under the age of 18.

This is an especially difficult issue to deal with, partly because it is hard for us to think of children doing such things, but also because it is not always easy to tell the difference between normal sexual exploration and abusive behaviour. Children, particularly in the younger age groups, may engage in such behaviour with no knowledge that it is wrong or abusive. For this reason, it may be more accurate to talk about sexually harmful behaviour rather than abuse.

It is important that we all have the information we need to recognise the warning signs of harmful sexual behaviour at an early stage and seek help. Every adult who cares about children can take responsibility for preventing abuse and ensuring that those involved have the help they need.

### What is healthy sexual development?

We all know that children pass through different stages of development as they grow, and that their awareness and curiosity about sexual matters change as they pass from infancy into childhood and then through puberty to adolescence.

Each child is an individual and will develop in his or her own way. However, there is a generally accepted range of behaviours linked to children's age and developmental stage. Sometimes these will involve some exploration with other children of similar age. It can be difficult to tell the difference between age-appropriate sexual exploration and warning signs of harmful behaviour. Occasionally we may need to explain to children why we would prefer them not to continue with a particular behaviour. This is a chance to talk with them about keeping themselves and others safe and to let them

know that you are someone who will listen.

Disabled children may develop at different rates, depending on the nature of their disability, and they can be more vulnerable to abuse. Children with learning disabilities, for example, may behave sexually in ways that are out of step with their age. Particular care may be needed in educating such children to understand their sexual development and to ensure that they can communicate effectively about any worries they have.

It is important to recognise that, while people from different backgrounds have different expectations about what is acceptable behaviour in children, sexual abuse happens across all races and cultures.

The section below shows some examples of normal and healthy sexual behaviour that we might expect to see in our children as they pass through different stages of development from pre-school to adolescence. Remember that each child develops at his or her own pace and not every child will show all these behaviours. This section also describes other behaviour that may give cause for concern. If you have any worries or questions about a child you know, talk to someone about it. Your health visitor, GP or child's teacher may be able to help, or you could ring the Stop it Now! Helpline.

### What is age-appropriate sexual behaviour?

Pre-school children (0-5 years) commonly:
⇨ Use childish 'sexual' language to talk about body parts
⇨ Ask how babies are made and where they come from
⇨ Touch or rub their own genitals
⇨ Show and look at private body parts.

They rarely:
⇨ Discuss sexual acts or use sexually explicit language

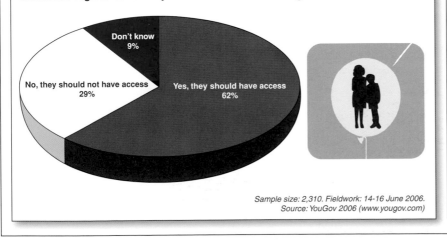

**Access to the child sex abuse register**

Respondents were asked: 'Do you think parents should have access to the child sex abuse register to identify child abusers in their neighbourhood?'

Don't know 9%

No, they should not have access 29%

Yes, they should have access 62%

Sample size: 2,310. Fieldwork: 14-16 June 2006.
Source: YouGov 2006 (www.yougov.com)

⇨ Have physical sexual contact with other children
⇨ Show adult-like sexual behaviour or knowledge.

School-age children (6-12 years) commonly:
⇨ Ask questions about menstruation, pregnancy and sexual behaviour
⇨ Experiment with other children, often during games, kissing, touching, showing and role-playing e.g. mums and dads or doctors and nurses
⇨ Masturbate in private.

---

## Sexually harmful behaviour by children and young people ranges from experimentation that unintentionally goes too far, through to serious sexual assault

---

Older children in this age range are also more likely than pre-school children to use sexual words and discuss sexual acts, particularly with their friends

They rarely:
⇨ Masturbate in public
⇨ Show adult-like sexual behaviour or knowledge.

Adolescents (13-16 years) commonly:
⇨ Ask questions about relationships and sexual behaviour
⇨ Use sexual language and talk about sexual acts between themselves
⇨ Masturbate in private
⇨ Experiment sexually with adolescents of similar age.

NB. About one-third of adolescents have sexual intercourse before the age of 16.

They rarely:
⇨ Masturbate in public
⇨ Have sexual contact with much younger children or adults.

### What is sexually harmful behaviour?

Sexually harmful behaviour by children and young people ranges from experimentation that

PREVENTION EDUCATION

unintentionally goes too far, through to serious sexual assault. It sometimes involves children as young as four or five, although most of those who sexually harm others are adolescents. Usually, but not always, the child or young person causing the harm is older than the victim. Often victims are uncomfortable or confused about what is happening and may feel that they are willingly involved, but not understand that the behaviour is harmful.

It is important to recognise that our children will engage in some forms of sexual exploration with similar-age children. However, any child or young person who engages in sex play with a much younger or more vulnerable child, or who uses force, tricks or bribery to involve someone in sexual activity, is a cause for concern and we should seek help or advice.

'The best way to keep your family safe is to educate yourself about child sexual abuse. The earlier we can see what is happening, the earlier we can do something to stop the abuse.' – The mother of a sexually abusing adolescent

### What about child pornography?

As well as the activities described above, we also have to be aware of the serious and growing problem of children and young people downloading sexual images of children on the internet. We do not know what effect looking at such material may have on their sexual and emotional development, but repeated viewing of child or adult pornography is certainly a cause for concern. In addition, downloading child pornography is a criminal offence. Young people who look at this material should be made aware that it is a crime and may need help with their behaviour. It is important that we keep a careful eye on what websites our children are visiting and restrict access as necessary. Further information and links are available on the Stop it Now! website: www.stopitnow.org.uk

### Why do some children sexually harm others?

The reasons why children sexually harm others are complicated and not always obvious. Some of them have been emotionally, sexually or physically abused themselves, while others may have witnessed physical or emotional violence at home. For some children it may be a passing phase, but the harm they cause to other children can be serious and some will go on to abuse children into adulthood if they do not receive help. For this reason it is vital to seek advice and help as soon as possible.

'I didn't have the words to tell my parents what was going on. I said I didn't want to be left alone with kids. I wish they had listened to me...' – A sexually abusing adolescent

⇨ The above information is an extract from the Stop It Now! document *Child's Play?* and is reprinted with permission. Visit www.stopitnow.org.uk for more information.

© Stop It Now!

# Sexual violence against children

## Shocking levels of sexual violence against children exposed

A report by Save the Children reveals horrific levels of sexual abuse and sexual exploitation of children across the world. The study brings together the voices of thousands of children across 13 countries on this highly sensitive issue.

Between 13 and 27 per cent of all children had suffered sexual abuse or exploitation.

In Canada, children make up 61% of the victims of sexual abuse.

In Nigeria, 16% of hospital patients treated for sexually transmitted infections were under 5 years old.

In Brazil up to 500,000 boys and girls are estimated to be involved in sexual exploitation.

As governments meet at the UN on 11 October to discuss whether to end violence against children, Save the Children is calling for a global ban on all violence – including sexual abuse and exploitation – committed against children. The need is urgent: 97 per cent of the world's children do not have the same legal protection against violence as adults.

Meena, child in Bangladesh, 'If one of the girls is sexually abused by a relative, adults in the family do not believe us. If a girl talks about the sexual abuse at home, she can be thrown out of home or she is treated so badly that she has to run away. If a girl is sexually abused where she works as the domestic worker, she is thrown out and the man who abuses her goes without any punishment.'

There is growing awareness that sexual violence is a crime. However, its secretive nature means vast numbers of sexual attacks on children are still going unreported, allowing the abuse to continue.

Jasmine Whitbread, CEO of Save the Children UK, 'It's inconceivable that children are not properly protected against the horrors of sexual violence. This survey underlines the shocking situation in 13 countries, yet it exposes only a small part of the picture. So much sexual abuse still goes unreported. We can only guess at the real levels children are being forced to endure across the world.'

Save the Children is calling for all governments to:
⇨ ban all forms of violence against children wherever they occur
⇨ create an effective national child protection system
⇨ establish a child-friendly juvenile justice system
⇨ mobilise men and boys in the battle to end violence against children
⇨ support the appointment of a special representative at the UN to drive forward the global project to end violence against children.

*6 October 2006*

⇨ The above information is reprinted with kind permission from Save the Children. Visit www.savethechildren.org.uk for more information.

# Online child abuse images

## IWF reveals 10-year statistics on child abuse images online

Marking its tenth anniversary, the Internet Watch Foundation (IWF) today revealed statistics and trends from a decade combating illegal online content. Since its inception in 1996, the organisation has processed an average of 1,000 reports a month with more than 31,000 websites found to contain potentially illegal child abuse content.

Its primary aim is to work in partnership at home and abroad with other hotlines to identify and remove potentially illegal child abuse content wherever it is hosted

in the world. From its origins as the only authorised UK 'Hotline' dealing with such material, at least 23 other countries now have a similar facility.

The outstanding success of the UK approach has seen the number of reported child abuse websites hosted in the UK rapidly decrease from 18% in its first year to 0.2% today.

The development of technology and increasingly sophisticated tracing methods have led to the IWF combating online child abuse content in areas such as online photo sharing services, message boards and proprietary groups as well as newsgroups and websites.

The statistics underline the need for unified international efforts, transcending borders and legal jurisdictions as well as the continuing need to raise the public's awareness of the 'Hotline's' work and the online reporting mechanism.

## Key IWF statistics and trends over the last 10 years

⇨ 615 reports processed in our first year, 27,750 reports processed in our tenth year

⇨ 18% of online child abuse images reported in our first year were hosted in UK whereas just 0.2% of online child abuse images reported in our tenth year were hosted in the UK

⇨ 79% of the child victims featured in the images are female

⇨ Of all reports processed over the period, 92% relate to web-based content and 7% to newsgroups

⇨ There is a 50/50 split between those who file reports anonymously and those who give their details. Of all reports processed:

⇨ 85% relate to suspected child abuse websites

⇨ 10% relate to suspected criminally obscene websites

⇨ 5% relate to incitement to suspected racial hatred websites. A third of all reported child abuse websites are confirmed by IWF to be potentially illegal.

Of all reported content confirmed to contain child abuse content over the past decade:

⇨ 51% appeared to be hosted in the US

⇨ 20% appeared to be hosted in Russia

⇨ 7% appeared to be hosted in Spain

⇨ 5% appeared to be hosted in Japan

⇨ 1.6% was hosted in the UK.

There has been a significant increase over the last twelve months in the severity of the abuse depicted on commercial child abuse websites.

Of commercial child abuse websites traced during the last 6 months and reported to Hotlines and law enforcement agencies around the world, 62% were removed within a month, 38% were still active after a month and 2% were still live after 6 months.

To raise awareness of its work, the organisation will reveal its full 10-year statistics and new intelligence in London on 24th October 2006. Home Office Minister, Vernon Coaker

MP, will address the 250 delegates including parliamentarians, teachers, child protection workers, police, local authorities, industry representatives, and IT professionals.

Home Office Minister, Vernon Coaker MP, said: 'I am delighted to mark the IWF's landmark campaign and pay tribute to its work over the past decade. The Government is determined to do everything it can to protect children from the insidious use of the internet by paedophiles.

'It is crucial to raise awareness amongst UK internet users about the IWF as a vehicle to report their inadvertent exposure to illegal content. This campaign underlines the importance of the work by the IWF and the ISPs to block UK residents from accessing potentially illegal websites, wherever they are hosted, by the end of 2007.'

Peter Robbins, IWF Chief Executive, said: 'Founded by the internet industry in 1996, the IWF has gone on to secure a membership of over 70 companies and organisations and has almost eradicated online child abuse images hosted in the UK.

'We are proud to share our successful self-regulatory model with other countries. Our achievements are testament to an outstanding partnership approach, securing support from the internet and mobile industry, public, Government and the police and many others, however, there is still important work to be

done in raising the public's awareness of our work so we can engage with other hotlines around the world to have these dreadful images of child abuse removed as quickly as possible. '

The conference event will be replicated in Birmingham, Manchester, Newcastle and Bristol and will coincide with advertising in each region. The new advertising can be seen on the IWF website: www.iwf. org.uk.

IWF would like to express its gratitude to Central Hall Westminster, Millennium Copthorne Hotels and Jurys Bristol Hotel for their generous support in providing the venues free of charge for the national conference events.

*24 October 2006*

⇨ The above information is reprinted with kind permission from the Internet Watch Foundation. The IWF is the only authorised organisation in the UK operating an internet 'hotline' for the public and IT professionals to report their exposure to potentially illegal content online. Their aim is to minimise the availability of potentially illegal internet content, specifically child abuse images hosted anywhere in the world; criminally obscene content hosted in the UK; and incitement to racial hatred content hosted in the UK. Visit www. iwf.org.uk for more information.

© *Internet Watch Foundation*

# What is grooming and online child abuse?

## Information from the Child Exploitation and Online Protection (CEOP) Centre

### What is child sex abuse?

A child sex abuser (commonly referred to as a paedophile) is someone who is sexually attracted to a child or children and acts upon those desires.

---

**A child sex abuser is sexually attracted to children and acts upon those desires**

---

### Why do child sex abusers like to use the internet to contact children?

Child sex abusers find the internet an easier place to participate in a range of child sexual abuse activity including contact with children due to the anonymity of the medium. They will often lie and pretend to be younger than they are or people other than themselves, and find a sense of security by operating from the safety of their own homes. They have been known to set up bogus email accounts and chat personas to mask their identity online.

### What are children at risk of, from child sex abusers, online?

There are a number of actions which these adults will engage in online. These include:

⇨ Swapping child abuse images in chat areas or through instant messenger with other adults or young people and forming networks with other child abusers to share tips on how to groom more effectively and how to avoid being caught.

⇨ Swapping personal information of children that they have collected with other abusers.

⇨ Participating in online communities such as blogs, forums and chat rooms with the intention to groom children, collect sexually explicit images and meet them to have sex.

### What is online grooming?

Online grooming is:

'A course of conduct enacted by a suspected paedophile, which would give a reasonable person cause for concern that any meeting with a child arising from the conduct would be for unlawful purposes.'*

Often, adults who want to engage children in sexual acts, or talk to them for sexual gratification will seek out young people who desire friendship. They will often use a number of grooming techniques including building trust with the child through lying, creating different personas and then attempting to engage the child in more intimate forms of communication including compromising a child with use of images and webcams. Child sex abusers will often use blackmail and guilt as methods of securing a meeting with the child.

You can make a report within the reporting section on the CEOP website.

*Sourced from www.netalert.net.au*

⇨ The above information is reprinted with kind permission from Child Exploitation and Online Protection (CEOP) Centre. Visit www.ceop.gov.uk for more information.

© CEOP

## The top ten

### Think u know . . .

1  It's best not to give out your personal details to online mates.
2  Personal stuff includes your messenger id, email address, mobile number and any pictures of you, your family or friends.
3  If you publish a picture or video online – anyone can change it or share it.
4  SPAM/ Junk email and texts: don't believe it, reply to it or use it.
5  It's not a good idea to open files that are from people you don't know. You won't know what they contain – it could be a virus, or worse – an inappropriate image or film.
6  It's easier to get on with people online and say stuff you wouldn't offline.
7  Some people lie online.
8  It's better to keep online mates online. Don't meet up with any strangers without an adult you trust. Better to be uncool than unsafe!
9  It's never too late to tell someone if something makes you feel uncomfortable.
10 There are people who can help. Report online child abuse, or find more advice and support.

⇨ The above information is reprinted with kind permission from the Child Exploitation and Online Protection (CEOP) Centre's 'ThinkUKnow' education campaign. Visit www.thinkuknow.co.uk for more information.

© CEOP

# False Memory Syndrome

## Information from the Child and Woman Abuse Studies Unit

### What is 'False Memory Syndrome'?

There is no medically, or clinically, recognised diagnosis of 'False Memory Syndrome'. The concept was invented in the USA by the False Memory Syndrome Foundation (FMSF), a group of 'accused parents' – mainly fathers – whose adult daughters had confronted them about sexual abuse in childhood. Having created this fictional concept of 'false memory' to defend themselves against these allegations, this group then went on to sell it to the media. The concept was imported to Britain from the US by Roger Scotford. Scotford set up the UK-based False Memory Syndrome Society, in response to being accused independently by two of his adult daughters of sexually abusing them. The British group also gained enormous coverage and support in the media.

> There is no medically, or clinically, recognised diagnosis of 'False Memory Syndrome'

The media's role has been crucial in enabling the FMSF, and its fellow organisations in other countries, to promote this invented 'syndrome' and to introduce it into public debate. For the media, the 'syndrome' provided a new spin on sexual abuse and journalists have played a critical part in giving credence to this pseudo-medical/psychological term, as with the term 'road rage'.

An American study found that between 1992 and 1994, following the founding of the FMSF, 85% of articles on child sexual abuse in leading magazines focused on false memories and false accusations. This contrasts with only 7% of articles during 1982-4.

Alongside the invention of 'FMS', those who promote it have also introduced the concepts of 'recovered memory therapy' and the 'recovered memory movement' neither of which exist. The origins of both can be found in *Making Monsters* (Richard Ofshe and Ethan Watters, 1995).

This text links disparate researchers, therapists and writers into spurious unity of purpose and perspective, despite the fact that they are not part of any organisation and express a diversity of views. The only thing that is common is that they all believe it is possible to forget traumatic experiences.

### Who coined the term 'False Memory Syndrome'?

Ralph Underwager, one of the founders of the False Memory Syndrome Foundation, is credited with having coined the term. In 1993, he gave an interview with the Dutch paedophile magazine, *Paedika*, in which he was reported as saying that paedophilia could be a responsible choice and that having sex with children could be seen as 'part of God's will'. The other co-founders of the FMSF were Pamela and Peter Freyd, whose adult daughter made accusations of childhood sexual abuse. The American media gave them almost unquestioning support until their daughter, psychology Professor Jennifer Freyd, felt obliged to speak out publicly, to stop the damage that she felt her parents and their organisation were doing to abuse survivors.

Other early promoters of false memory syndrome in the US were Paul and Shirley Erberle. In the 1970s, when child pornography laws were less rigid, they edited a magazine called *Finger* in which there were explicit illustrations of children involved in sexual acts with adults, with features entitled 'Sexpot at Five', 'My First Rape, She Was Only Thirteen' and 'Toilet Training'. Another key figure is Felicity Goodyear-Smith, author of *First Do No Harm* (1993). Felicity Goodyear-Smith admits to a personal as well as professional involvement in the issue. Her husband and parents-in-law were imprisoned for sexual abuse offences, having been members of the New Zealand community, CentrePoint, that encouraged sexual intimacy amongst its members, including the children. Although the adults involved were prosecuted for these acts, including public sex with

children, Goodyear-Smith claims that this was simply 'childhood sexual experimentation' and quotes studies that claim to show that adult-child sex can be harmless.

## Is there any evidence that amnesia occurs as a result of trauma?

Research has demonstrated that a significant proportion of adults with documented evidence of being sexually abused in childhood 'forget' or block out the abuse – even when they have been treated in hospital as a result of it, or have been through a successful prosecution of the perpetrator in court. The clinical term for this kind of 'forgetting' is 'dissociation' – which is, unlike 'false memory syndrome', a medically recognised diagnosis. Dissociation occurs after trauma, as a result of the brain's mechanisms for storing overwhelming emotional and physiological experience. Dissociation as a response to trauma has been found in soldiers who have survived combat and accident victims who have 'blocked out' the event.

Scheflin and Brown (1996) conducted a meta-analysis of scientific literature on amnesia or repressed memory of child sexual abuse. They found that amnesia as a result of child sexual abuse is a robust finding across studies using very different samples and measures of assessment. Linda Williams (1995) followed up 129 women who, 17 years earlier as children, had been admitted into a hospital emergency room for sexual assault. As adults, 38% did not recall the abuse. The 62% who did recall the abuse did so with accounts that were 'remarkably consistent with the evidence' from the hospital.

The accounts of the women who had always remembered were no more or less consistent than those of the women who had 'forgotten' and then recovered the memories. Both types of remembering were found to be reliable.

Feldman-Summers and Pope (1994) surveyed 500 psychologists. 25% of women and 6% of men reported an experience of sexual abuse in childhood. 40% had 'forgotten' some or all of the experience, and for only a quarter of this group was therapy the only factor in remembering. Forgetting was more common where abuse began in early childhood, took place over a longer period; was perpetrated by a relative and involved more forms of violation. Half of those reporting abuse had found corroboration from other relatives; court or medical records; journals and diaries or a confession by the abuser.

Two further studies have asked if survivors had forgotten for any length of time: in Briere and Conte's (1993) sample of 450 adult survivors over half (59%) said that they had 'forgotten' for a considerable period of time; in Herman and Schatzow's (1987) smaller sample of women almost two-thirds (63%) also said that they had 'forgotten' for some time. Only 6% of the latter group could find no corroboration of their abuse.

In *Children Who Don't Speak Out* Radda Barnen (Swedish Save the Children) reports on a study of children who were identified through seizures of child pornography. None of them had told anyone about their abuse. The researchers compared the children's statements, the contents of the seized pornography and the statements of the abusers. All of the children resisted remembering the abuse. They spoke only about incidents which were recorded on the pornography when prompted and some even denied that the recorded abuse had happened. The abusers were as, if not more, reticent in their statements, admitting only to what there was forensic evidence about.

## What about therapists who have been found guilty of planting 'false memories'?

There has been no malpractice suit in which a case against a practitioner on this issue has been upheld. A much more significant problem is the number of therapists who have sexual relationships with vulnerable clients who are seeking help following sexual assault. A number of malpractice suits have been upheld involving this form of abuse.

## Can FMS be a result of hypnotherapy?

None of the named cases publicised by the UK FMSS have involved adults recovering memories through hypnotherapy. An examination of FMSS files by an independent organisation found that adults who FMSS claimed have had 'false memories' belonged to one of the following categories:

⇨ they had always believed that they were sexually abused;

⇨ they began to remember in adulthood as a result of some external trigger in their lives, outside the context of therapy. In one famous case an adult (Jennifer Freyd) did some short-term work with a clinical psychologist, and another (Scotford's daughter) with a homeopath. Neither had hypnotherapy or so-called 'regression' therapy at any point.

Given all of this evidence the basic question must be why so many people are more comfortable believing in false memories than the accounts of adults and children.

⇨ The above information is reprinted with kind permission from the Child and Woman Abuse Studies Unit. Visit www.cwasu.org for more information.

© *London Metropolitan University*

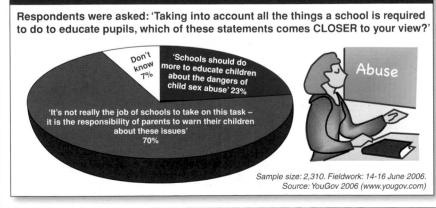

**Education about child sex abuse**

Respondents were asked: 'Taking into account all the things a school is required to do to educate pupils, which of these statements comes CLOSER to your view?'

Don't know 7%

'Schools should do more to educate children about the dangers of child sex abuse' 23%

'It's not really the job of schools to take on this task – it is the responsibility of parents to warn their children about these issues' 70%

Abuse

Sample size: 2,310. Fieldwork: 14-16 June 2006.
Source: YouGov 2006 (www.yougov.com)

# Help for abusers

## New report reveals many sexual abusers willing to seek help

A report published by Stop It Now! UK and Ireland reveals that 45% of calls to its Helpline are from people concerned about their own sexual thoughts, feelings and behaviours towards children. A further 35% of calls are from friends and family concerned about the sexual behaviour of someone close to them.

The first report on the Stop It Now! Helpline highlights key findings of groundbreaking work carried out by the Helpline over three years (2002-2005), and concludes that a radical review is needed of how child sexual abuse is portrayed and tackled in our communities.

The Internet Watch Foundation supports the work of Stop It Now! and welcomes their report. Tink Palmer of Stop It Now! is a member of the IWF Board of Trustees.

Operation of the confidential Freephone Helpline commenced in June 2002.

It is aimed at:

⇨ Men and women worried about their own sexual thoughts, feelings and behaviours towards children

⇨ Men and women worried about the sexual attitudes and behaviour of someone close to them

⇨ Parents and carers worried about the sexual behaviour of a child or young person.

### Key findings for the period June 2002-May 2005

1 Total number of calls – 4013; total number of callers – 2076.

2 Total number of calls made by abusers and potential abusers concerned about themselves – 1804. This represents 45% of all calls to the Helpline. 676 (16%) of these calls were concerned with the misuse of the Internet.

3 Total number of calls made by friends and family concerned about another adult's behaviour – 1190. This represented 30% of total calls.

4 Total number of calls from parents, carers and other adults concerned about a child or young person's behaviour – 204. This represented 5% of all calls.

### Calls by abusers and potential abusers (not related to Internet concerns)

Abusers and potential abusers call the Helpline in ever increasing numbers. The majority are concerned about their sexual thoughts and behaviour towards a child within their own family. The Helpline assists them to identify one or more steps they can take to manage their thoughts and to ensure immediate and future safety of the child.

---

**45% of calls to its Helpline are from people concerned about their own sexual thoughts, feelings and behaviours towards children**

---

### Calls made by Internet offenders and potential Internet offenders

Over the three years the Helpline has experienced a dramatic increase in calls concerning the misuse of the Internet to view child pornography or to sexually groom children. Those concerned about their own behaviour are often desperate to escape what they see as an addiction. Their family and friends are also desperate to establish the likelihood of immediate risk to children within the family and to find a way of restoring trust in the future.

### Calls made by family and friends

The most typical family or friend caller is a female concerned about the sexual attitudes or behaviour of her partner or child. The Helpline assists her to judge the nature and extent of risk and offers ongoing support in taking steps to keep her own and other children safe.

### Call for action

*'The scale of the problem of the sexual abuse of children is such that a major rethink of policy is needed – with greater emphasis on prevention and early intervention.'* Joseph Rowntree Foundation, 2004

Baroness Valerie Howarth of Breckland, OBE, says:

'It is extremely difficult for people to recognise that their own behaviour or that of someone very close to them may be sexually abusive. It is a mark of true success that so many people have felt able to seek and receive advice through the Stop it Now! Helpline.'

Donald Findlater, Deputy Director of the Lucy Faithfull Foundation and Manager of the Stop it Now! Helpline says:

'Over the past three years we have learned that adults will call and get help to prevent the sexual abuse of a child. This includes those worried about their own sexual thoughts or behaviour towards children, as well as their loved ones.'

Tink Palmer of Stop it Now! UK and Ireland says:

'The current public climate discourages reporting, maintains silence and disables members of the community from seeking help or acting to protect children from abuse. Stop it Now! gives adults the information they need to prevent child sexual abuse. The Stop it Now! Helpline supports these adults to take protective action, often in circumstances unknown to police or social services.'
6 June 2006

⇨ The above information is reprinted with kind permission from the Internet Watch Foundation. Visit www.iwf.org.uk for more information.

© Internet Watch Foundation

# 'They're not monsters'

**Why would anyone want to spend time with high-risk sex offenders and become the object of hatred themselves? Yvonne Roberts meets the volunteers who are seeking to rehabilitate paedophiles with a mixture of love and support**

Laurence is a retired headteacher; Karen, in her 20s, is jobless; David is a grandfather and works for a charity; Tim, 29, is employed in IT. They are diverse in interests, outlook and background, but what links them is that they have volunteered to have regular contact with people whom many of us shun, fear and despise: high-risk sex offenders. They are, as one tabloid crudely put it, 'paedo-pals'.

But what kind of person takes responsibility, unpaid and with few thanks, for men and women who may revolt and repel? How do Laurence, Karen, David and Tim rationalise giving so much time and effort to abusers rather than the abused?

The organisation to which these four belong is Circles of Support and Accountability, based on a Canadian project that is now 10 years old. In 2002, the Home Office set up three pilot schemes in the UK, adapting the Canadian model. The pilots now number 105 trained volunteers, including housewives, a farmer, engineers and a former ballet teacher. Today, one of those pilots, the Thames Valley and Hampshire project, established by the charity Quaker Peace and Social Witness, receives a major award from the Howard League for Penal Reform for its efforts. So far, Thames Valley Circles has achieved an extraordinary degree of success. The project has helped 25 convicted paedophiles at high risk of causing serious harm. None has committed a new sexual offence. Without Circles, the risk of offending in this group, within a short time of leaving prison, is assessed at 60% by the Home Office.

Chris Wilson, a probation officer, has been project manager from the outset, heading a team of five. 'We can't afford to lock up every sex offender for life and we don't have the resources to rely on police

and probation to provide 24-hour surveillance,' he points out. 'Some offenders will never respond to support in the community but for others, Circles is effective.'

---

## What kind of person takes responsibility, unpaid and with few thanks, for men and women who may revolt and repel?

---

But it is also unpopular in some quarters. 'Kill the Paedophiles', reads one of the posters carried by children in demonstrations on the Paulsgrove Estate in Portsmouth, soon after Circles was established. The *News of the World* 'named and shamed' paedophiles as part of its campaign to have American legislation, 'Megan's Law', introduced here as 'Sarah's Law', in memory of eight-year-old Sarah Payne, murdered by a convicted paedophile. Megan's Law allows individuals to check a local register to see if a convicted offender lives in the neighbourhood.

The hatred that many feel for sex offenders was demonstrated by the killing of convicted paedophile Arnold Hartley in 2003, and the recent outrage over the sentencing of another, Craig Sweeney. And yet the Circles volunteers are convinced that what they are doing is worthwhile. Working in groups of three or four, they will meet an offender formally each week for a year – and informally for an indeterminate time. In the worst cases, or when imprisonment disrupts the process, offenders may go through a number of circles. Supported by a professional coordinator, the volunteers encourage the offender to jettison delusions

and self-justifications and become accountable for his or her behaviour. All information, meanwhile, is shared with professionals including police, probation and other services.

David became a volunteer four years ago, partly because of his faith as a Quaker and partly because of his belief in 'restorative justice'. Restorative justice means that the community accepts a responsibility for the reintegration of offenders – on moral grounds and to prevent further victims, some of whom could themselves become paedophiles. 'If I can stop anybody harming a child, then that's of value to me,' David says.

David's 'circle' includes a professional hypnotherapist and a person working with the homeless. 'As volunteers, you make friends with people you would never otherwise have met,' David says. 'That's one of the rewards.' The circle's 'core member' – the offender, in other words – is Sam, 23. Sexually abused by older girls from the age of five, as a teenager he was sentenced to five years for sexual assault. He now works in a supermarket, has a girlfriend, and is developing a social life – activities that the circle encourages but also views as opportunities to reoffend.

David sees himself as both supporter and watchdog. 'I'm committed to Sam's wellbeing,' he says, 'but if he did anything to cause me concern, I'd have no compunction in taking action.

'One core member came to us saying that he could manipulate anybody. We turned it round and told him, "You're only in a position to manipulate us if we let you. That's not your power – it's ours.' The relationship between the volunteers and how they gel is critical."

As well as the formal meetings, volunteers also meet core members informally, going to the cinema or for a coffee, to demonstrate how 'normal' adult relationships are conducted.

Offenders are often isolated, rejected by family and friends, socially inadequate and suffering from low self-esteem. Research says that a paedophile living in this kind of dehumanised social exile is much more likely to offend again.

That is a message confirmed by Harry – divorced, with two daughters, and a convicted paedophile. 'I sometimes wonder what life would have been like had I not been accepted into Circles,' he says. 'Pretty bleak! Without Circles I would seldom leave the flat and would be prey once more to depression and paranoia. But I have been able to discuss and relate stuff about my past life, my feelings towards children and many other things that until now I have kept to myself. I really feel I have made more progress in understanding myself and my offending than I did throughout all the years in prison or on the sex offender treatment programmes, essential though they were.'

John is in his 50s, and one of David's core members. Abused as a child, he went on to abuse his sister and then his daughters until the eldest was 21. He served several years in prison. 'John was the first sex offender I had knowingly met and I liked him,' David says. 'He was outgoing and pleasant, but in the first few meetings he went through his story and I remember thinking, "How could you do this to a child?"

'Since then, I've come to see core members not as sex offenders and "monsters" but as people – electricians, plumbers, Man U supporters, whatever – who have also committed sexual offences. There is a difference: one view denies someone's humanity, the other affirms it. John discovered that however badly he acted, however much he tried to shock us volunteers, we didn't walk away. He has changed out of all recognition.'

Three years on, John is studying for a degree in creative writing. He sees his circle informally – and he is moving into tricky waters. 'He is in a relationship with a woman who has a daughter and grandchildren,' David explains. 'She knows about his past and the circle has insisted that he discloses it to all her family. It's difficult but that's what he's now doing.'

How can he be sure that John is not practising the paedophile's art of deception? 'I can't,' David replies, 'but volunteers talk to each other. One may pick up what the others don't and we can always talk to the coordinators.'

'What we're looking for in volunteers are people who can separate the person from the behaviour,' Chris Wilson says. 'Individuals who can empathise but not sympathise. We constantly reinforce the message, "Think the unthinkable, imagine the unimaginable." Even as the risk escalates, volunteers may go into denial, because of their disbelief that the core member could do that after so much effort has been invested. But they can and do. So we manage circles carefully and offer booster training. Along the way, we have achieved major little miracles.'

How would David cope if a core member did something dreadful, in spite of his vigilance? 'I wouldn't carry the guilt,' he says. 'It's his choice. All I can do is help him not make that choice and take action if he causes concern.'

How does he justify the support given to core members rather than victims? 'I've worked in children's services enough to know some who have been abused never recover, while a core member can rebuild his life. I would put a lot more money into support circles adapted for survivors, too. But what I also believe is that Circles is about prevention – no more victims.'

In four years, three core members have been recalled to prison on licence because of a circle's concern about likely recidivism. One of them was grooming girls in internet chat rooms. Another four offenders have been 'called to account' by the Circle for behaviour causing concern, such as 'inappropriate' sexual activities with a fellow hostel member. In these cases, monitoring was increased.

'If a core member is recalled to prison, volunteers can feel they've failed,' says project coordinator Rebekah Saunders. 'But we point out that, from a public protection point of view, what they've done is clearly a success.'

Karen became a volunteer nine months ago because she thought it might complement the psychology degree she begins in the autumn. 'You're asked to sign up for a year,' she says, 'but you soon discover that you're in it for life. Circles has that effect.' The core member of Karen's circle is Peter, a serial offender, in his 60s and with a low IQ. His story illustrates how volunteers' vigilance can never flag.

Peter was electronically tagged and placed in a probation hostel on his release because of the likelihood that he would reoffend and possibly murder a child. He was in denial about his offences. After a year in his first circle, his personal hygiene, confidence and appearance had improved. He had a job as a cleaner and he had moved to sheltered accommodation. He spent Christmas Day with one of his circle. He reported that it was the best he had ever had.

The second and third year taught Circles a lesson. Among other issues, Peter had coerced a man into buying a car on his behalf. He had previously used a car to abduct a child. Volunteers also learned that Peter had invited young girls to his flat, contravening the terms of his release. Nothing had yet occurred but Peter was given a community sentence and returned to a supervised hostel. Karen is one of Peter's second circle. She goes to the pub to watch him in his darts team. 'It's brilliant – not children!' she says. 'He often hides his limited understanding,' she adds. For instance, he was told not to go within 50 metres of a school as part of his sex offender order but when asked, he didn't really know what 50 metres meant. We had to show him. And keep showing him, because he doesn't retain much.

'He's a likable chap so you have to constantly remind yourself why he's in the circle. People say to me that they've never talked to an offender, but they probably have. They've just haven't realised.' Would she tell a friend with children if a core member moved in next door? 'That's an interesting dilemma,' she answers. 'It would depend on how the core member is behaving and who the friend is. The bottom line is: no more victims.'

In 2004/5, there were 28,994 registered sex offenders, an 18% increase over the previous year. Many offenders will be on the register for life. They are assessed, monitored and managed under 'multi-agency public protection arrangements' (Mappas), involving agencies including police, probation and the prison service as well as housing, health and social services. Each offender's risk of reoffending is assessed using psychometric evaluation, some polygraph testing and a range of assessment tools that endeavour to gauge critical issues such as distorted attitudes towards sex; self-discipline and relationship skills.

Three levels of risk exist. Level one is the lowest and involves supervision by a single agency such as probation; three is the highest. Level-three offenders – the 'critical few', 1,478 in number – pose the highest risk of causing serious harm. Circles draw their core members from levels two and three.

Laurence, 65, is a retired head-teacher. He is in his fifth circle. 'Most offenders can't believe we're in the circle because we want to be, not because it's our job,' he says. Among Laurence's core members is Harry, who served six years of an eight-year sentence for assaulting the nine-year-old friend of his youngest daughter. For the first nine months of the circle, he denied his culpability and saw his actions with the girl, now 15, as 'love', imagining they would be reunited when she became an adult.

'We didn't seem to be getting very far because Harry said little about his feelings,' Laurence says. 'Then he revealed that he had kept a diary. He said he was worried, it would corrupt me. I assured him that it wasn't my poison. The diary was gruesome. It revealed a paedophile who had virtually ignored his own daughters. I told him they must be feeling awful. I told him to take down the photographs of the victim that he had on his wall, and that his behaviour was ridiculous.' Harry eventually took down the photographs. He and his daughters and circle members subsequently met for a meal at which the younger daughter began to cry. 'I'm so happy,' she said. 'We've got our dad back.'

In managing sex offenders, of course, there is no guaranteed happy ending – least of all for the victims of their abuse. Like many volunteers, Laurence is careful whom he tells about his work with Circles. 'The initial reaction is always, "Oh my God, how could you?" Ten minutes later, almost 100% say it's a fantastic idea. They soon grasp that an "us and them" attitude just doesn't protect victims.'

Tim, the IT man, says he joined Circles partly from a selfish motivation. 'It looks good on my CV if I develop my knowledge of "soft skills" – how to motivate, how to develop non-judgemental questioning. But at the same time, the idea that we should castrate all sex offenders clashes with my personal morality. It doesn't seem a very practical solution to the issue.'

He is now in his second circle. 'It wouldn't surprise me if a core member does eventually commit a serious crime – and it might be murder,' he says candidly. 'We can't stop all sex offending. What circles are about is significantly reducing the risk. That has to matter.'

Wilson has now helped to establish circles in several areas of the UK, including Manchester, Somerset, York and Norfolk. The Thames Valley project costs £250,000 a year. The saving in suffering to potential victims, of course, is incalculable. The project has been evaluated twice using Home Office measures and judged a success.

The Thames Valley project has 14 high-risk sex offenders waiting for a circle – but funding is uncertain beyond next year. Supporters say more resources and more volunteers are desperately required so that Circles can become an effective part of every community, anchoring sex offenders securely above ground, monitored and stripped of camouflage. Sarah's Law, they argue, will only drive paedophiles further into the dark, multiplying the number of victims. 'Circles do provide a community response,' David points out. 'They apply the positive values of compassion, tolerance, kindness and self-discipline. For the health of the whole community that has to work better than vengeance, intolerance and hate.'

⇨ Some names have been changed.
*11 July 2006*

# KEY FACTS

⇨ Some children are not loved by their families. Others live in families that are having a really difficult time and cannot cope with their problems. Some children are deliberately neglected or hurt by the adults around them. (page 1)

⇨ In 2001/02, ChildLine counselled over 112,000 children about all kinds of problems and concerns. 21,000 of children counselled (20 per cent) rang about physical or sexual abuse, sometimes both. (page 2)

⇨ There are laws to protect children and to deal with people who abuse them. The most important laws are the Children Act 1989 (England and Wales), the Children (Scotland) Act 1995 and the Children (Northern Ireland) Order 1995. (page 3)

⇨ Children are usually abused by someone in their immediate family circle. This can include parents, brothers or sisters, babysitters or other familiar adults. It is quite unusual for strangers to be involved. (page 4)

⇨ Of children surveyed who said they grew up feeling unloved, one in ten (11%) became suicidal; more than a quarter (28%) were depressed; and one in four (27%) were unable to concentrate in school. (page 5)

⇨ More than 1.25 billion children – over half of the world's child population – can still legally be beaten by their teachers in school. (page 7)

⇨ 85 per cent of adults surveyed agreed that 'parents should sometimes be allowed to smack their children'. (page 8)

⇨ Public opinion polls tell us that 85-90 per cent of the general public supports the use of mild physical correction as a form of discipline. (page 14)

⇨ Corporal punishment is lawful in the home, though the defence of 'reasonable chastisement' has been limited by amendments to the law in England and Wales and in Scotland. English common law has allowed parents and others who have 'lawful control or charge' of a child to use 'moderate and reasonable' chastisement or correction. (page 15)

⇨ One in seven parents in this country smack their children. (page 18)

⇨ Most children surveyed (43 out of 76) described a smack as 'a hit', 'a hard hit' or 'a very hard hit'. Only one child described a smack as being a 'pat', though she quickly added 'only harder'. (page 19)

⇨ 27% of people surveyed by Ipsos MORI believed child sex abuse should be punished by death. 42% believed it should be punished with a life sentence. (page 24)

⇨ Eighty two per cent of children surveyed by the NSPCC did not realise it is illegal for a 30 year old man to sexually touch a 15 year old girl. (page 27)

⇨ 89% of those surveyed by YouGov believed sentences for child sex abusers were too lenient. (page 28)

⇨ A third of those who have sexually abused a child are themselves under the age of 18. (page 29)

⇨ 62% of those surveyed by YouGov believed parents should have access to the child sex abuse register to identify child abusers in their neighbourhood. (page 29)

⇨ Between 13 and 27 per cent of all children across the world had suffered sexual abuse or exploitation, according to a report by Save the Children. (page 31)

⇨ 18% of online child abuse images reported to the Internet Watch Foundation in 1996 were hosted in the UK whereas just 0.2% of online child abuse images reported in 2006 were hosted in the UK. (page 32)

⇨ Child sex abusers find the Internet an easier place to participate in a range of child sexual abuse activity including contact with children due to the anonymity of the medium. They will often lie and pretend to be younger than they are or people other than themselves, and find a sense of security by operating from the safety of their own homes. They have been known to set up bogus email accounts and chat personas to mask their identity online. (page 33)

⇨ There is no medically, or clinically, recognised diagnosis of 'False Memory Syndrome'. The concept was invented in the USA by the False Memory Syndrome Foundation (FMSF), a group of 'accused parents' – mainly fathers – whose adult daughters had confronted them about sexual abuse in childhood. (page 34)

⇨ 70% of those surveyed by YouGov believed that 'It is not really the job of schools to take on this task [of educating children about the dangers of child sex abuse] – it is the responsibility of parents to warn their children about these issues.' (page 35)

⇨ A report published by Stop it Now! UK and Ireland reveals that 45% of calls to its Helpline are from people concerned about their own sexual thoughts, feelings and behaviours towards children. A further 35% of calls are from friends and family concerned about the sexual behaviour of someone close to them. (page 36)

# GLOSSARY

**Abuse**
To treat someone with cruelty or violence.

**Corporal punishment**
Physical punishment, inflicted with hands or implements. In the UK, corporal punishment is legal in the home (and usually takes the form of smacking), although it must fall into the category of 'reasonable chastisement'.

**Emotional abuse**
Emotional abuse is when children do not feel loved or valued because they are constantly told off, put down or told they are not good at anything. When children are emotionally abused, they are turned away when they need love or support, and are frequently rejected or ignored by those who are meant to look after them.

**Grooming**
Online grooming is defined as a course of conduct enacted by a suspected paedophile, which would give a reasonable person cause for concern that any meeting with a child arising from the conduct would be for unlawful purposes. Often adults who want to engage children in sexual acts or talk to them for sexual gratification will seek out young people who desire friendship. They will often use a number of grooming techniques including building trust with the child through lying, creating different personas and then attempting to engage the child in more intimate forms of communication.

**Neglect**
Neglect is when children are denied the essentials in life they need to grow up and become healthy, well-cared-for adults. Neglected children are forced to get by without proper food, housing, medical care or clothing.

**Paedophile**
A person who is sexually attracted to children.

**Physical abuse**
Physical abuse is when a child is hurt by being smacked, hit, or shaken; beaten by hand, with a belt or other objects; or physically abused in other ways.

**Sexual abuse**
Sexual abuse is when a child takes part in sexual activities, whether or not the child is aware of what is happening. Abusers are not usually strangers, but a relative, friend of the family, lodger, babysitter or someone at school. Sexual abuse is usually carried out by men, but sometimes women do it too.

**Smacking**
Smacking is the most common form of corporal punishment in the home and is legal in the UK. One in seven parents smack their children, according to a recent survey. However, some people feel that it is a form of child abuse and should be made illegal.

# INDEX

# Additional Resources

## Other Issues titles

If you are interested in researching further some of the issues raised in *Child Abuse*, you may like to read the following titles in the **Issues** series:

⇨ Vol. 125 *Understanding Depression* (ISBN 978 1 86168 364 9)
⇨ Vol. 124 *Parenting Issues* (ISBN 978 1 86168 363 2)
⇨ Vol. 123 *Young People and Health* (ISBN 978 1 86168 362 5)
⇨ Vol. 122 *Bullying* (ISBN 978 1 86168 361 8)
⇨ Vol. 120 *The Human Rights Issue* (ISBN 978 1 86168 353 3)
⇨ Vol. 108 *Domestic Violence* (ISBN 978 1 86168 328 1)
⇨ Vol. 104 *Our Internet Society* (ISBN 978 1 86168 324 3)
⇨ Vol. 99 *Exploited Children* (ISBN 978 1 86168 313 7)
⇨ Vol. 77 *Self-inflicted violence* (ISBN 978 1 86168 266 6)

For more information about these titles, visit our website at www.independence.co.uk/publicationslist

## Useful organisations

You may find the websites of the following organisations useful for further research:

⇨ Child Exploitation and Online Protection Centre (CEOP): www.ceop.gov.uk
⇨ ChildLine: www.childline.org.uk
⇨ End All Corporal Punishment of Children: www.endcorporalpunishment.org
⇨ Family Education Trust: www.famyouth.org.uk
⇨ Internet Watch Foundation: www.iwf.org.uk
⇨ ITV: www.itv.com
⇨ NSPCC: www.nspcc.org.uk
⇨ Raising Kids: www.raisingkids.co.uk
⇨ Royal College of Psychiatrists: www.rcpsych.ac.uk
⇨ Save the Children: www.savethechildren.org.uk
⇨ TheSite.org: www.thesite.org
⇨ Stop It Now!: www.stopitnow.org.uk
⇨ YouGov: www.yougov.com
⇨ Young Minds: www.youngminds.org.uk

# ACKNOWLEDGEMENTS

The publisher is grateful for permission to reproduce the following material.

While every care has been taken to trace and acknowledge copyright, the publisher tenders its apology for any accidental infringement or where copyright has proved untraceable. The publisher would be pleased to come to a suitable arrangement in any such case with the rightful owner.

### Chapter One: Child Abuse

*Child abuse*, © ChildLine/NSPCC, *Child abuse and neglect*, © Royal College of Psychiatrists, *One child in ten grows up feeling unloved*, © NSPCC, *Coming to terms with abuse*, © TheSite.org, *Corporal punishment in schools*, © Save the Children.

### Chapter Two: The Smacking Debate

*The smacking debate*, © ITV, *'It never did me any harm…'*, © Global Initiative to End All Corporal Punishment of Children, *A human rights issue*, © Global Initiative to End All Corporal Punishment of Children, *Against a smacking ban*, © Family Education Trust, *Smacking ban rejected*, © Raising Kids, *Lawfulness of corporal punishment*, © Global Initiative to End All Corporal Punishment of Children, *Child discipline*, © ITV, *Most parents smack*, © Raising Kids, *It hurts you inside*, © Save the Children.

### Chapter Three: Child Sex Abuse

*Abuse*, © Young Minds, *Child sexual abuse*, © London Metropolitan University, *Education on sexual abuse*, © NSPCC, *Getting over sexual abuse*, © TheSite.org, *Child's play?*, © Stop It Now!, *Sexual violence against children*, © Save the Children, *Online child abuse images*, © Internet Watch Foundation, *What is grooming and online child abuse?*, © CEOP, *Top ten tips*, © CEOP, *False Memory Syndrome*, © London Metropolitan University, *Help for abusers*, © Internet Watch Foundation, *'They're not monsters'*, © Guardian Newspapers Ltd 2006.

### Photographs and illustrations:

Pages 1, 12, 25, 32: Simon Kneebone; pages 7, 13, 30, 34: Angelo Madrid; pages 9, 18, 27, 39: Don Hatcher; pages 11, 22: Bev Aisbett.

And with thanks to the team: Mary Chapman, Sandra Dennis and Jan Haskell.

Lisa Firth
Cambridge
January, 2007